SAS for Windows Workbook

for

Tabachnick and Fidell
Using Multivariate Statistics
Fourth Edition

D1716562

Barbara G. Tabachnick
California State University, Northridge

Allyn and Bacon
Boston London Toronto Sydney Tokyo Singapore

ISBN 0-205-32785-0

Printed in the United States of America

10 9 8 7 6 5 4 3 2 1   03 02 01 00

TABLE OF CONTENTS

LIST OF FIGURES

LIST OF OUTPUT

SAS for Windows Workbook

to Accompany *Using Multivariate Statistics*

Preface

This workbook demonstrates analysis of the complete examples of *Using Multivariate Statistics* (Tabachnick and Fidell, 1996) through SAS for Windows. This is not meant to be a stand-alone publication, but rather is to be used in conjunction with the text--only material specific to SAS for Windows is demonstrated here. Data files are available on the publisher's Website for the book on the Internet: http://www.abacon.com/Tabachnick.

I thank Linda Fidell, my co-author of the text, for her friendship, inspiration, and general good cheer. She is all that one could want in a collaborator, colleague and friend. And I'd like to thank my husband, Ken, for his patience, continuing support, and even his editorial comments.

Barbara G. Tabachnick

Chapter 1. Introduction

The first three chapters of *Using Multivariate Statistics* (*UMS*) introduce basic concepts and review univariate and bivariate statistics; they contain no complete examples. In order to maintain the same chapter numbering as in the text, Chapter 2 of this workbook is a brief guide to the techniques covered in Chapters 4 through 16. Chapter 3 is an overview of SAS for Windows and reviews some basics for retrieving SAS system files into SAS for Windows, and for creating SAS system files from ASCII data files.

This workbook assumes a familiarity with the Windows environment and the use of Help facilities within Windows programs. Data sets used in this workbook are SAS system files, entitled *fname*.SAS7BDAT and are available on the publisher's Website for the book on the Internet: http://www.abacon.com/Tabachnick. All of the data sets for this workbook are contained in a single executable file: SAS_UMS.EXE.

Each chapter in this workbook begins with a brief description of the applicable data file. Chapters 4 through 16 of the workbook are meant to be used at a computer with SAS for Windows loaded and ready to go, and with *UMS* firmly in hand, opened to the complete example(s) near the end of the corresponding chapter.

Appendix B of *UMS* provides further information about the variables in the data sets. The version of SAS for Windows used to produce this workbook is 7.0, running under Windows 98. The workbook also is compatible with version 8.0. It is assumed that the reader is familiar with Windows, as well as with some general procedures using SAS for Windows, such as use of the Program Editor, Output, and Log windows.

Chapter 2. A Guide to Techniques

This workbook follows the format of the accompanying text, *Using Multivariate Statistics*. Chapter 4 of the workbook provides setups and output for screening ungrouped and grouped data sets from Chapter 4 of *UMS*. That chapter is referred to often in the remaining chapters and presents techniques in greater detail, so it is a good idea to work through the chapter before proceeding to any of the others. Chapter 5 provides setups and output for standard and hierarchical multiple regression. Chapter 6 demonstrates canonical correlation. Chapter 7 shows how to do hierarchical loglinear analysis. Chapter 8 shows analysis of covariance. Chapter 9 demonstrates setups and outputs for multivariate analysis of variance and covariance examples. Chapter 10 shows profile analysis of repeated measures as well as doubly multivariate repeated measures ANOVA. Chapter 11 shows an example of direct discriminant function analysis. Chapter 12 demonstrates direct logistic regression analysis with two outcomes and sequential logistic regression with three outcomes. Chapter 13 shows how to do a principal factor analysis. Chapter 14 shows structural equation modeling. Chapter 15 shows survival analysis and Chapter 16 demonstrates a time series analysis.

Many of the complete examples in *UMS* are demonstrated with statistical programs in packages other than SAS. The computer runs in this workbook are meant to correspond as closely as possible to those of the syntax and output in the text.

Chapter 3. Overview of SAS for Windows

SAS for Windows does all of the basic univariate and bivariate analyses: analysis of variance, correlation and regression, and produces many varieties of plots. Many of the basic procedures for univariate and bivariate statistics are reviewed in Chapter 4 of this workbook, in the context of screening grouped and ungrouped data sets, and in other chapters in the context of requirements for specific multivariate analyses.

Some statistical procedures are unavailable through dialog boxes: discriminant analysis, factor analysis, and structural equation modeling, for example. For other procedures, such as regression, the number of variables available through the graphical interface is limited. Section 3.5 shows how to use batch files in SAS for Windows.

SAS is unique in the variety of different ways to accomplish a task. In addition to the choice between batch and graphical approaches to statistical procedures, for example, there are at least three ways to view files, as seen in the next section.

3.1 CREATING YOUR OWN SAS LIBRARY

The first thing you may want to do is create a folder to hold the SAS system files that you create (.SAS7BDAT files) and that you copy from those made available on

disk or on the Internet to accompany this workbook.

You might consider putting the .SAS7BDAT files into a folder that is easy to back up, for example D:\MYFILES if you routinely back up your D:\ partition. You then create a SAS library and direct it to the folder you have created or to the disk. (The default SASUSER library is neither easy to find nor handy to back up.) Say, for example, you want to create a library called BTFILES and locate it in your D:\MYFILES\ folder. To create the library, locate the **Add new library** icon on the SAS menu bar (Figure 3.1) and click on it.

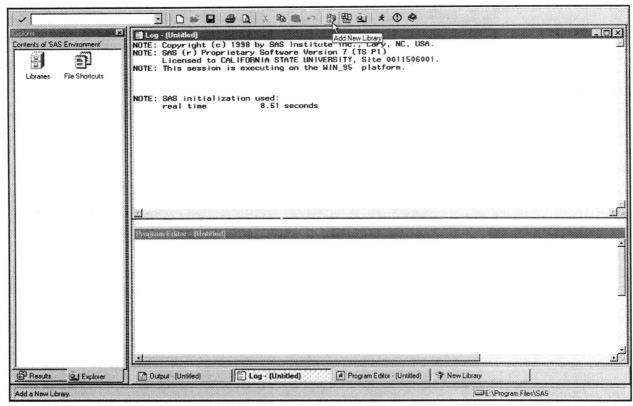

Figure 3.1   **Add New Library** icon.

This produces the **New Library** dialog box, into which you enter your library name and path, as seen in Figure 3.2.

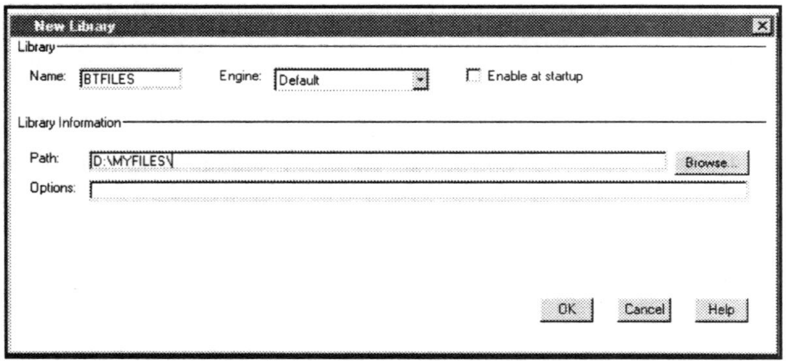

Figure 3.2   **New Library** dialog box.

You may then copy the *.SAS7BDAT files into your folder (e.g., D:\MYFILES\) using your usual Windows methods.

You also may copy the files from your folder into the default SASUSER location through SAS Explorer if you like. SAS Explorer is located at the left of the main SAS screen (see Figure 3.1), where double clicking on the **Libraries** icon shows all of your libraries, as seen in Figure 3.3.

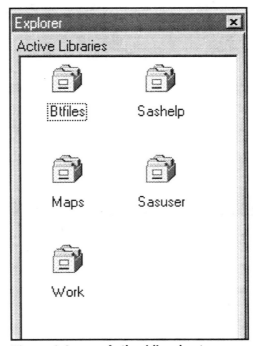

Figure 3.3   **Active Libraries** icons.

Double clicking on icons shows all of the files in a library, and you can use the usual Windows Copy and Paste to copy files from one library to another. Files will be extracted from the SASUSER library for the remainder of this workbook.

3.2   SAS ASSIST

SAS ASSIST provides the graphical interface to SAS procedures such as data management and statistics without typing SAS instructions explicitly. Figure 3.4 shows the **Solutions** menu, in which you select **ASSIST** to produce the for the graphical SAS interface, shown in Figure 3.5.

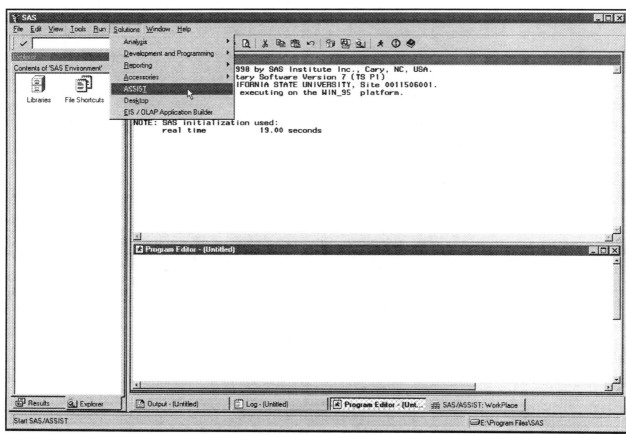

Figure 3.4   **Solutions** menu to choose **ASSIST**.

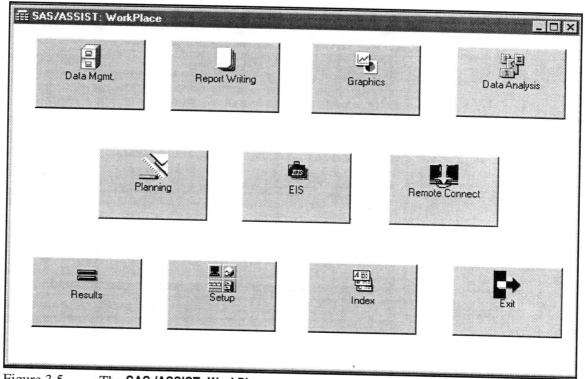

Figure 3.5   The **SAS /ASSIST: WorkPlace.**

Statistical procedures are selected by clicking on the **Data Analysis** button.

3.3   VIEWING FILES IN SAS

3.3.1   Using ASSIST to View Files

The files on the disk that accompanies this workbook are SAS system files. They contain data in SAS "*fname*.SAS7BDAT" format (not ASCII format), and include data definitions as well as values. For example the file, SCREEN.SAS7BDAT, provides data values and definitions for the Chapter 4 examples of data screening. These files cannot be viewed or edited outside of SAS. SAS system files are retrieved for analysis into SAS for Windows within the analysis instructions. However, they and other types of files, such as ASCII files, may be viewed and edited as part of the data management procedure. For example, from the **SAS/ASSIST: WorkPlace** menu of Figure 3.5, clicking on the **Data Mgmt.** button produces the menu of Figure 3.6.

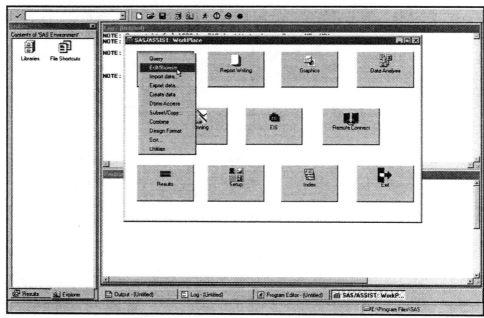

Figure 3.6   The **Data Mgmt.** menu

Clicking on

> **> Edit/Browse**
> **> Browse Data...**

produces the submenu of Figure 3.7, and then the **Browse Data** dialog box of Figure 3.8.

Figure 3.7   **Edit/Browse**
submenu.

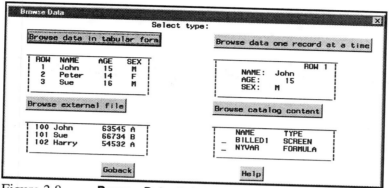

Figure 3.8   **Browse Data** dialog box.

Here you can choose to look at different kinds of files in various formats. For example, clicking on the **Browse external file** button brings up the **SAS/ASSIST: Browse an External File** dialog box (Figure 3.9), where you type in the path and file name for the file you want to look at, here the comma delimited ASCII (text) file SCREEN.CSV.

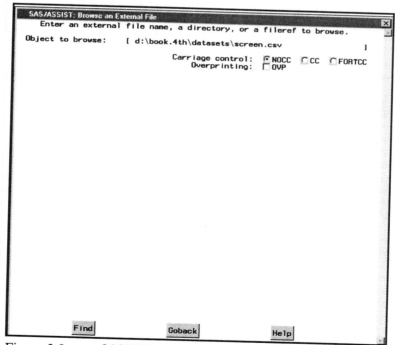

Figure 3.9   **SAS/ASSIST: Browse an External File** dialog box.

Pressing the **Enter** key on the keyboard shows the file on the screen, as seen in Figure 3.10.

```
FSLIST: d:\book.4th\datasets\screen.csv
SUBNO,TIMEDRS,ATTDRUG,ATTHOUSE, INCOME,EMPLMNT,MSTATUS,RACE
1,1,8,27,5,1,2,1
2,3,7,20,6,0,2,1
3,0,8,23,3,0,2,1
4,13,9,28,8,1,2,1
5,15,7,24,1,1,2,1
6,3,8,25,4,0,2,1
7,2,7,30,6,1,2,1
8,0,7,24,6,1,2,1
9,7,7,20,2,1,2,1
10,4,8,30,8,0,1,1
11,15,9,15,7,1,2,1
12,0,6,22,3,1,2,1
13,2,6,19,5,1,2,1
14,13,8,25,6,1,2,1
15,2,5,17,1,1,2,1
16,2,8,19,3,0,2,2
21,1,8,22,1,1,2,1
22,2,6,21,7,0,1,1
23,5,8,28,2,1,2,1
24,5,10,25,9,0,2,1
25,3,6,19,4,0,2,1
26,4,5,31,5,0,2,1
```

Figure 3.10   Viewing a comma-delimited ASCII file.

Remove this window from the screen by clicking the ⊠ icon at the upper right. Then work your way back to the **SAS/ASSIST: WorkPlace** by clicking on the **Goback** and **Exit** buttons of the various dialog boxes and menus that appear.

3.3.2   Opening Files into the Program Editor

Another, simpler, way to view any text file, including a data file, is by simply opening a file in the typical Windows fashion:

> **File**
> > **Open...**

The usual Windows **Open** dialog box then appears, and selecting a file puts it into the **Program Editor**, as seen in Figure 3.11.

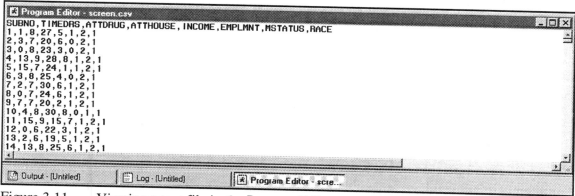

Figure 3.11   Viewing a text file in the **Program Editor**.

3.3.3   Interactive Data Analysis

The **Interactive Data Analysis** module is another handy way to view data files that are in SAS format (*.SAS7BDAT), and allows you to create and edit them as well. The module is entered from the main menu bar of Figure 3.4 by choosing

> > <u>S</u>olutions
> >   > Anal<u>y</u>sis
> >   > <u>I</u>nteractive Data Analysis

This produces the **SAS/Insight: Open** list box which prompts you to choose a file from one of your SAS libraries, for example the SASUSER directory, as seen in Figure 3.12.

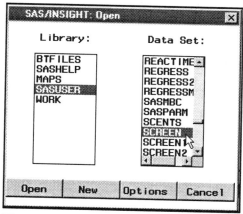

Figure 3.12   **SAS/Insight: Open** list box.

13

Clicking on the desired file name, here SCREEN, and then **Open** brings the file into a spreadsheet-like window, as seen in Figure 3.13.

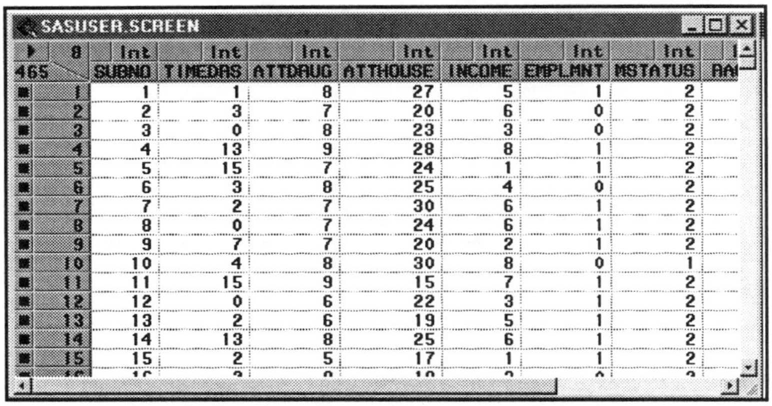

8	Int	Int	Int	Int	Int	Int	Int	
465	SUBNO	TIMEDRS	ATTDRUG	ATTHOUSE	INCOME	EMPLMNT	MSTATUS	RA
1	1	1	8	27	5	1	2	
2	2	3	7	20	6	0	2	
3	3	0	8	23	3	0	2	
4	4	13	9	28	8	1	2	
5	5	15	7	24	1	1	2	
6	6	3	8	25	4	0	2	
7	7	2	7	30	6	1	2	
8	8	0	7	24	6	1	2	
9	9	7	7	20	2	1	2	
10	10	4	8	30	8	0	1	
11	11	15	9	15	7	1	2	
12	12	0	6	22	3	1	2	
13	13	2	6	19	5	1	2	
14	14	13	8	25	6	1	2	
15	15	2	5	17	1	1	2	

Figure 3.13   Data window for interactive data analysis.

Use of **Interactive Data Analysis** for data screening is illustrated in Chapter 4.

3.4   CREATING SAS FILES FROM ASCII DATA FILES

The files on the disk that accompanies this workbook are SAS system files, containing variable definitions as well as data. However, you may have data in ASCII (text) files, containing data values alone as in Figure 3.11. These files are imported through

> **File**
> > **Import Data...**

which supports a variety of data formats, including .CSV (comma delimited) files as shown in Figures 3.10 and 3.11, files with variables separated by blanks, spreadsheet files, databases, and the like. Files also may be imported through the **Data Mgmt.** facility of the **SAS/ASSIST: WorkPlace** of Figure 3.5, but that is quite a bit more complex.

14

3.5   MISSING DATA

SAS assumes that all missing data are indicated by a period (.). This is the missing value code in all of the SAS data files used in this workbook, because with large data sets it sometimes is easier to recode values in ASCII files outside of SAS for Windows using, for example, a word processing program or editor. In SAS for Windows, the easiest ways to change data values are through a batch file or manually in an **Interactive Data Analysis** session as is illustrated in Section 4.1.3.

3.6   BATCH FILES

You may find yourself with batch files of SAS instructions (in ASCII format) from a non-Windows implementation of SAS, such as a DOS, VAX, or UNIX version. SAS for Windows processes these files from the **Program Editor,** the bottom window in Figure 3.1, where the procedures of Section 3.3.2 bring the file into the editor.

Or you may find that an analytic technique is not implemented or is only partially implemented in the SAS/ASSIST menu system. A new set of batch instructions may be typed into the **Program Editor** window. The text file of instructions is saved by selecting from the main menu:

> > <u>F</u>ile,
> >   > <u>S</u>ave as....

The usual Windows dialog box then opens for naming and locating the file to be saved.

Instructions also are generated when SAS ASSIST dialogs are run. These can be cut from the **Log** window (the top window in Figure 3.1) and pasted into the **Program Editor** window, and then edited to be run as a batch file.

In any event, clicking on the icon showing a person running (to be referred to in this workbook as the runner icon) on the toolbar submits the batch job. The log file appears in the **Log** window as the run is executed. Figure 3.14 shows a log for a batch file.

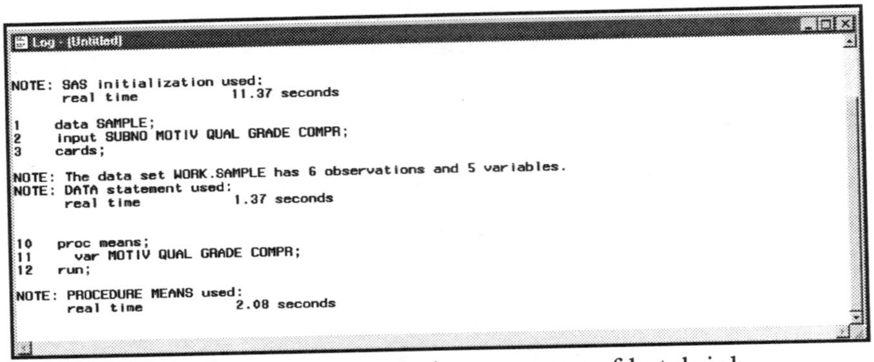

Figure 3.14 **Log** window showing progress of batch job submitted.

If the run is successful, results appear in a full screen window entitled **Output**, as seen in Figure 3.15. The following section shows how to print or save this or any other output to a file.

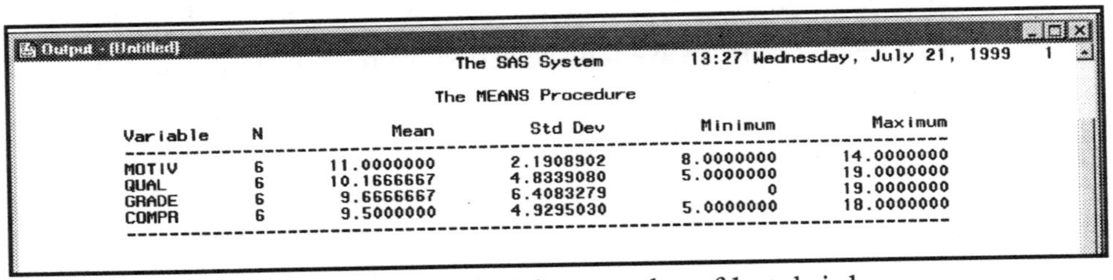

Variable	N	Mean	Std Dev	Minimum	Maximum
MOTIV	6	11.0000000	2.1908902	8.0000000	14.0000000
QUAL	6	10.1666667	4.8339080	5.0000000	19.0000000
GRADE	6	9.6666667	6.4083279	0	19.0000000
COMPR	6	9.5000000	4.9295030	5.0000000	18.0000000

Figure 3.15 **Output** window showing results of batch job.

3.7 VIEWING AND PRINTING RESULTS OF DATA ANALYSIS

Often after running a data analysis procedure the output appears on screen for viewing, printing, or saving. (Sometimes you need to open the window from the list of windows at the bottom of the SAS screen, or even select **Output** from the **View** menu on the main SAS taskbar of Figure 3.4.) Output from any SAS window is printed or saved from the main taskbar, with

> **File**
>> **Save As...**

which produces the usual Windows dialog boxes for saving files.

Printing or saving a file also is accomplished from the main taskbar with

> **File**
> > **Print....**

You are then led through dialog boxes to choose the file to be printed and whether you want the output (or other window) to be printed to a file instead of sent to the printer. Note that unless you blank out the current output, subsequent output will be appended to the output window.

Chapter 4. Data Screening

This chapter demonstrates data screening for ungrouped and grouped data using SAS/ASSIST in SAS for Windows, for the complete examples of Chapter 4, *Using Multivariate Statistics*. The SAS data file to use is SCREEN.SAS7BDAT.

The first example evaluates distributions and relationships among six variables that are to be treated as continuous in multivariate analyses such as multiple regression, canonical correlation, or factor analysis. Variables are attitudes toward use of medication (ATTDRUG), attitudes toward housework (ATTHOUSE), INCOME, current marital status (MSTATUS), RACE, and visits to health professionals (TIMEDRS).

The second example looks at distributions and relationships among these six variables separately by groups formed by current employment status (EMPLMNT). The six variables are to be treated as continuous in such multivariate analyses as multivariate analysis of covariance or discriminant function analysis.

4.1   SCREENING UNGROUPED DATA

4.1.1   Histograms and Descriptive Statistics for Initial Screening

Histograms and descriptive statistics are found in SAS for Windows through the **Interactive Data Analysis** procedure, accessed as per Section 3.3.3. Choosing from the taskbar:

> **Analyze**
> > **Distribution (Y)**

produces the **Distribution (Y)** dialog box of Figure 4.1 for choosing variables.

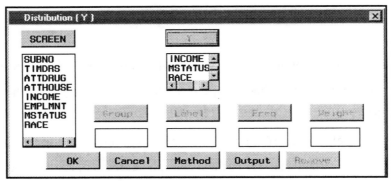

Figure 4.1   **Distribution (Y)** dialog box.

Choose the variables you want by clicking on them and then on the **Y** button. All variables except SUBNO and EMPLMNT are to be selected; recall that SUBNO is the subject identification variable and EMPLMNT is not used for the ungrouped data screening. (If you accidentally select a variable, just click on the **Cancel** button and try again.) Clicking on the **Output** button produces a dialog box (Figure 4.2) that allows you to choose the descriptive statistics you want. Here, the default Box Plots and Quantile statistics have been deselected, leaving only ☑**Moments** (descriptive statistics) and ☑**Histogram/Bar Chart.**

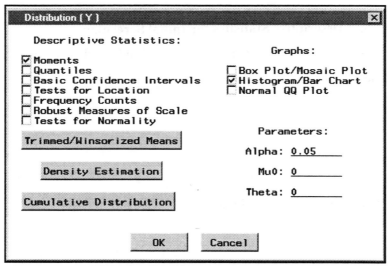

Figure 4.2   **Distribution (Y)** output dialog box.

Clicking on **OK** returns the dialog box of Figure 4.1, where clicking on **OK** produces a window with the histograms and descriptive statistics. Scrolling through the window shows the information for the variables, in turn, as seen in Figures 4.3 to 4.8.

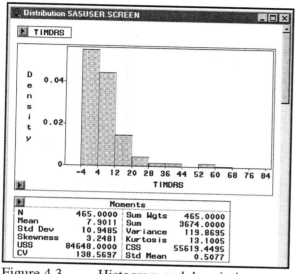

Figure 4.3   Histogram and descriptive statistics for TIMEDRS.

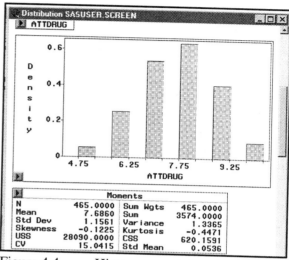

Figure 4.4   Histogram and descriptive statistics for ATTDRUG.

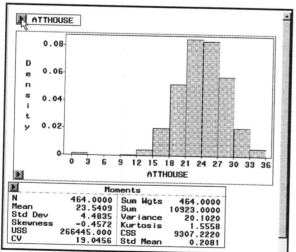

Figure 4.5   Histogram and descriptive statistics for ATTHOUSE.

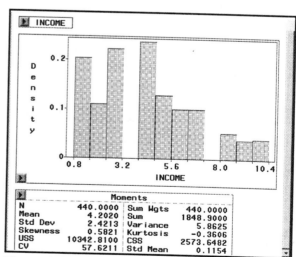

Figure 4.6   Histogram and descriptive statistics for INCOME.

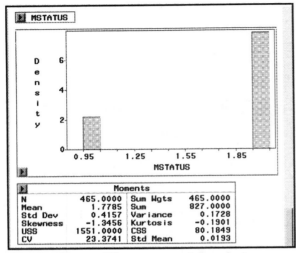

Figure 4.7   Histogram and descriptive statistics for MSTATUS.

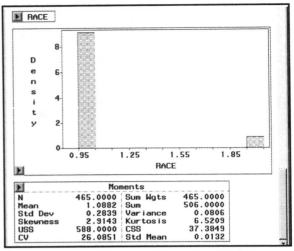

Figure 4.8   Histogram and descriptive statistics for RACE.

Missing values are not explicitly noted in this display, however they can be calculated by subtracting the displayed **N** from the actual number of cases read into the file (465 for this data set).

Choosing

> <u>F</u>ile
   > <u>S</u>ave
      > <u>T</u>ables

puts the numeric results into the SAS **Output** window, where it may be saved to a file or printed. *Output 4.1* displays a portion of that output.

Output 4.1 SAS INTERACTIVE DATA EXPLORATION OUTPUT SHOWING A PORTION OF DESCRIPTIVE STATISTICS FOR UNGROUPED DATA.

TIMDRS

		Moments	
N	465.0000	Sum Wgts	465.0000
Mean	7.9011	Sum	3674.0000
Std Dev	10.9485	Variance	119.8695
Skewness	3.2481	Kurtosis	13.1005
USS	84648.0000	CSS	55619.4495
CV	138.5697	Std Mean	0.5077

22

```
                        ATTDRUG

                        Moments
       N            465.0000    Sum Wgts      465.0000
       Mean           7.6860    Sum         3574.0000
       Std Dev        1.1561    Variance       1.3365
       Skewness      -0.1225    Kurtosis      -0.4471
       USS        28090.0000    CSS          620.1591
       CV            15.0415    Std Mean       0.0536
```

An alternative procedure for finding descriptive statistics is available. In the **SAS/ASSIST: WorkPlace** (Figure 3.5) choose

> **> Data Analysis**
>   **> Elementary**
>   **> Summary Statistics...**

This produces the **SAS/ASSIST: Summary Statistics** dialog box of Figure 4.9.

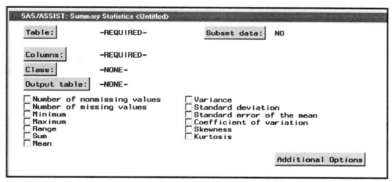

Figure 4.9   **SAS/ASSIST: Summary Statistics** dialog box.

Clicking on the **Table:** button produces a list of files in a **SAS/ASSIST: Select Table** window, where SASUSER.SCREEN is chosen as seen in Figure 4.10. (Note that SAS uses "table" to indicate a data set.)

23

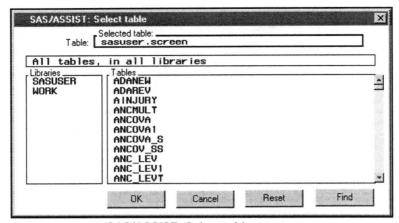

Figure 4.10   **SAS/ASSIST: Select table** window.

Clicking on **OK** returns the summary statistics window of Figure 4.9.

Clicking on the **Columns:** button produces the **Select Table Variables** window of Figure 4.11, where all variables except SUBNO and EMPLMNT are selected. (Note that "column" is used by SAS/ASSIST to indicate a variable.)

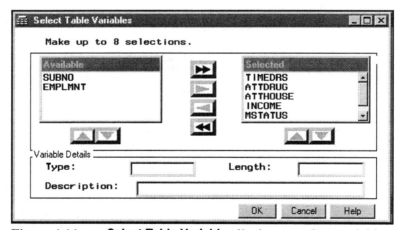

Figure 4.11   **Select Table Variables** list box to select variables for summary statistics.

Clicking on **OK** returns the summary statistics dialog box of Figure 4.9, where the statistics chosen are

> **SAS/ASSIST: Summary Statistics**
> ☑ **Number of nonmissing values**
> ☑ **Number of missing values**
> ☑ **Minimum**
> ☑ **Maximum**
> ☑ **Mean**
> ☑ **Variance**
> ☑ **Standard deviation**
> ☑ **Skewness**
> ☑ **Kurtosis**

as indicated in Figure 4.12.

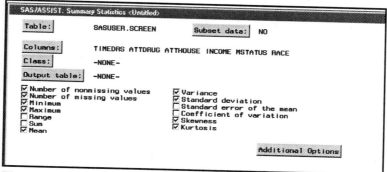

Figure 4.12   **SAS/ASSIST: Summary Statistics** dialog box with chosen statistics indicated.

Clicking on the runner icon (𝄆) produces *Output 4.2*.

Output 4.2 SAS/ASSIST SUMMARY STATISTICS OUTPUT.

The MEANS Procedure

Variable	Label	N	N Miss	Minimum	Maximum	Mean
TIMEDRS	Visits to health professionals	465	0	0	81.0000000	7.9010753
ATTDRUG	Attitudes toward use of medication	465	0	5.0000000	10.0000000	7.6860215
ATTHOUSE	Attitudes toward housework	464	1	2.0000000	35.0000000	23.5409483
INCOME	Income code	439	26	1.0000000	10.0000000	4.2095672
MSTATUS	Current marital status	465	0	1.0000000	2.0000000	1.7784946
RACE	Ethnic affiliation	465	0	1.0000000	2.0000000	1.0881720

Variable	Label	Variance	Std Dev	Skewness
TIMEDRS	Visits to health professionals	119.8695032	10.9484932	3.2481170
ATTDRUG	Attitudes toward use of medication	1.3365499	1.1560925	-0.1225099
ATTHOUSE	Attitudes toward housework	20.1019913	4.4835244	-0.4571589
INCOME	Income code	5.8509585	2.4188755	0.5815867
MSTATUS	Current marital status	0.1728124	0.4157071	-1.3456476
RACE	Ethnic affiliation	0.0805710	0.2838503	2.9142607

Variable	Label	Kurtosis
TIMEDRS	Visits to health professionals	13.1005155
ATTDRUG	Attitudes toward use of medication	-0.4470689
ATTHOUSE	Attitudes toward housework	1.5558403
INCOME	Income code	-0.3593650
MSTATUS	Current marital status	-0.1900686
RACE	Ethnic affiliation	6.5209440

As seen in the output, this corresponds to PROC MEANS in syntax.

Univariate outliers may be assessed by calculating standard scores (z scores) for maximum and minimum values for each variable. Alternatively, syntax may be used to create standard scores and view their maximum and minimum values, using SAS PROC STANDARD and PROC MEANS as per Table 6.9 of *UMS*.

4.1.2   Histogram and Descriptive Statistics with Outliers Deleted

Figure 4.5 shows the univariate outliers with very low scores on ATTHOUSE. Deletion of outliers is accomplished through **Interactive Data Analysis** by choosing:

> **E**dit
>> **O**bservations
>>> **E**xclude in Calculations
>>>> ATTHOUSE = 2

This produces the **Exclude Observations** dialog box, in which you click on ATTHOUSE, then =, and then 2, as seen in Figure 4.13 Note that although Figure 4.5 does not show exact values for outliers, Figure 4.13 does list all of the values, making it evident that the outlier(s) have a value of 2.

26

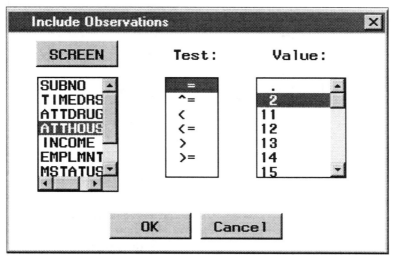

Figure 4.13   **Exclude Observations** dialog box.

Clicking on **OK** allows you to follow the same procedure to exclude outliers from the histogram by choosing

> **Edit**
>> **Observations**
>>> **Hide in Graphs**

and following the procedure for excluding observations in calculations (Figure 4.13) in the **Hide Observations** window that appears.

Once the missing value is replaced with the mean, following the procedure of Figure 4.1 (with only ATTHOUSE chosen) produces a modified histogram and set of descriptive statistics, as seen in Figure 4.14.

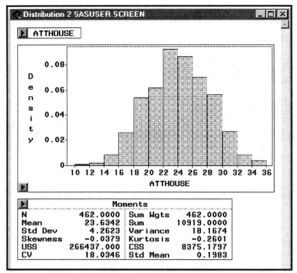

Figure 4.14   Descriptive statistics for
               ATTHOUSE with outliers
               deleted.

4.1.3   Replacing a Missing Value with the Mean

There is no straightforward way to recode values in **SAS/ASSIST**. The simplest way to replace a missing

value with the mean in **Interactive Data Exploration** is to scroll through the data set for a missing data (.)

indicator and manually insert the value. Click on the data value, type in 23.634, and then press **Enter** on

the keyboard. The descriptive statistics window automatically adjusts to the new value, as seen in Figure

4.15. Section 4.1.5 shows how to save the new data file.

SASUSER.SCREEN

465	SUBNO	TIMDRS	ATTDRUG	ATTHOUSE	INCOME	EMPLMNT
241	322	14	9	30.000	2.0	1
242	323	2	9	32.000	1.0	0
243	324	4	7	21.000	3.0	0
244	325	8	8	19.000	10.0	1
245	326	3	8	24.000	4.0	1
246	327	10	8	28.000	1.0	1
247	328	21	10	28.000	10.0	1
248	329	6	7	29.000	7.0	1
249	330	58	7	29.000	4.0	0
250	335	12	8	23.000	4.0	0
251	336	5	7	26.000	1.0	0
252	337	2	9	22.000	1.0	0
253	338	2	6	23.634	5.0	0
254	339	4	7	25.000	6.0	1
255	340	2	7	19.000	5.0	1

ATTHOUSE

Moments

N	465.0000	Sum Wgts	465.0000
Mean	23.5411	Sum	10946.6340
Std Dev	4.4787	Variance	20.0587
Skewness	-0.4578	Kurtosis	1.5657
USS	267003.566	CSS	9307.2306
CV	19.0250	Std Mean	0.2077

Figure 4.15 Data set and descriptive statistics with mean inserted for missing value on ATTHOUSE.

Alternatively, a batch file may be used to recode values, putting the recoded data into a new file (SASUSER.SCREENR), as per Figure 4.16. This procedure may also be used to change numerical missing value codes to the SAS system-missing code (.).

Program Editor - screenr.sas

```
data SASUSER.SCREENR;
  set SASUSER.SCREEN;
  if ATTHOUSE = . then ATTHOUSE = 23.6342;
run;
```

Figure 4.16 Batch file to replace a missing ATTHOUSE value with the mean.

4.1.4　Plots for Linearity and Homoscedasticity

Choosing

> **Analyze**
> > **Scatter Plot (Y X)**
> > > Y　ATTDRUG
> > > X　TIMEDRS

produces the **Scatter Plot (Y X)** dialog box of Figure 4.17. Clicking on ATTDRUG and then the **Y** button and then TIMEDRS and the **X** button selects the dependent and independent variables for the scatterplot.

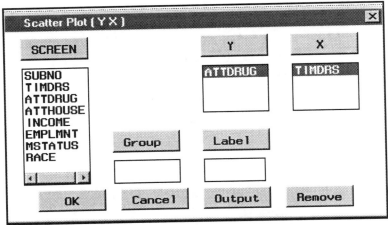

Figure 4.17　**Scatter Plot (Y X)** dialog box.

Clicking on **OK** produces the scatterplot in Figure 4.18.

30

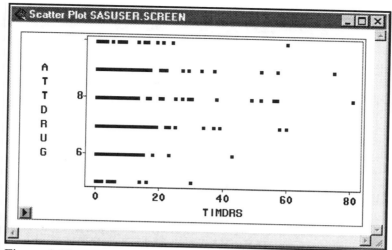

Figure 4.18   Scatterplot of ATTDRUG vs. TIMEDRS.

4.1.5   Transformation

The transformation of TIMEDRS to improve normality, linearity, and homoscedasticity is accomplished by choosing

> **> Edit**
>   **> Variables**
>   **> log (Y)**
>   **Y**   **TIMEDRS**
>   **Transformation::**   **log10(Y + a)**
>   **a:**   **1**
>   **Name:**   **LTIMEDRS**

produces the **Edit Variables** dialog box, in which TIMEDRS is selected as the **Y** variable. The transform **log10(Y + a)** is chosen from **Transformation:** list. The dialog box also is edited by replacing the 0 in **a:** with 1, as seen in Figure 4.19. This allows transformation of a variable that includes values of 0. You may also edit the **Name:** box so that the new variable (log of TIMEDRS + 1) is called LTIMEDRS in the data set. Clicking on **OK** creates the new variable.

31

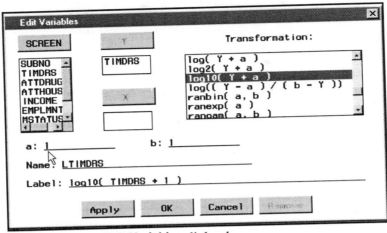

Figure 4.19   **Edit Variables** dialog box.

Outliers on ATTHOUSE must be excluded following procedures in Section 4.1.2 before producing the new histograms and descriptive statistics. Procedures in Figure 4.1 and 4.2 are then followed, selecting only LTIMEDRS, to produce the modified histogram and descriptive statistics shown in Figure 4.20.

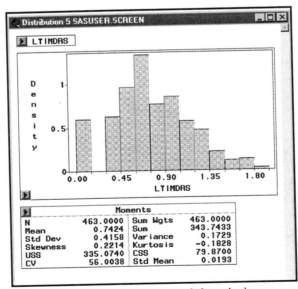

Figure 4.20   Histogram and descriptive statistics for LTIMEDRS.

Figure 4.21 plots the bivariate scatterplot between ATTDRUG and LTIMEDRS, produced by the same procedures used for the scatterplot between ATTDRUG and TIMEDRS, above (Section 4.1.4).

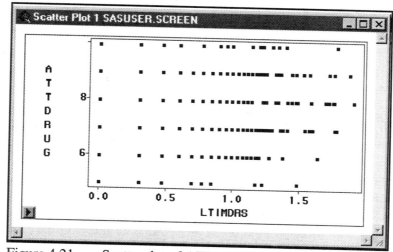

Figure 4.21   Scatterplot of ATTDRUG vs. LTIMEDRS.

The data set containing LTIMEDRS (with the missing value on ATTHOUSE replaced by the mean) may be saved by choosing

> **File**
>   > **Save**
>   > **Data...**
>   Data Set: **SCREEN1**

This produces the **Save Data** dialog box of Figure 4.22 to enter the new data set name (here SCREEN1). Alternatively, you may choose the same data set name, adding LTIMEDRS to the existing data set. (Under some circumstances SAS won't let you save the file under the same name.) Choosing the **SASUSER** library ensures that the file is saved permanently.

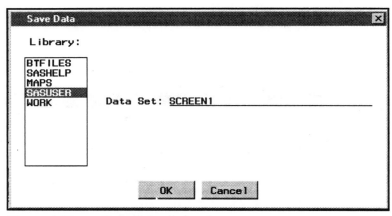

Figure 4.22   **Save Data** dialog box.

Not all transformations are available through **Interactive Data Analysis,** but instead may require syntax. An example of such a transform (where a new variable is created by dividing an existing variable by a constant) is in Section 15.1 of this workbook.

4.1.6   Multivariate Outliers through Regression

In the **SAS/ASSIST: WorkPlace** (Figures 3.4 and 3.5), selecting

>**Data Analysis**
>>**Regression**
>>>**Linear...**

produces the **SAS/ASSIST: Regression Analysis** dialog box of Figure 4.23.

34

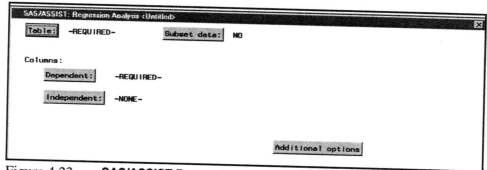

Figure 4.23   **SAS/ASSIST Regression Analysis** dialog box.

Clicking on the **Table:** button produces a list of files in the **SAS/ASSIST: Select Table** window (Figure 4.10), where SASUSER.SCREEN1 is chosen. Clicking on **OK** returns the regression analysis dialog box.

Clicking on the **Subset data:** button of the regression window produces the **Subset Data** dialog box (Figure 4.24), which allows exclusion of univariate outliers on ATTHOUSE.

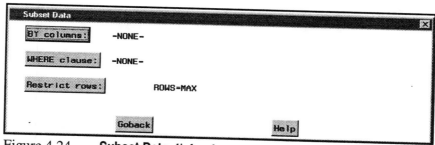

Figure 4.24   **Subset Data** dialog box.

Clicking on the **WHERE clause:** button produces the **Build a WHERE Clause to Subset the Current Data** dialog box of Figure 4.25 to select cases to analyze.

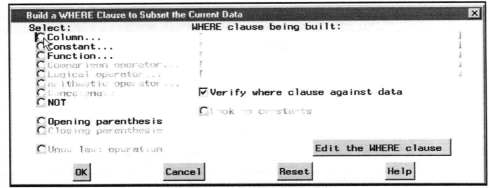

Figure 4.25   **Build a WHERE Clause to Subset the Current Data** dialog box.

Clicking on ⊙**Column...** produces a list that allows selection of ATTHOUSE. Clicking on ⊙**Comparison operator...** produces a list that allows you to choose ^= to indicate "not equal to", and clicking on **Constant...** produces a box in which you type in the number 2. Clicking on **Edit the WHERE Clause** produces Figure 4.26, in which the selection clause may be checked and edited if necessary. Clicking on **OK** and then **Goback** returns the **SAS/ASSIST: Regression Analysis** dialog box of Figure 4.19.

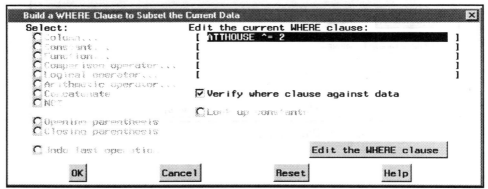

Figure 4.26   Displaying the WHERE clause.

Clicking on the **Dependent:** button produces the **Select Table Variables** list of Figure 4.27, where SUBNO is selected as the dummy DV (since multivariate outliers and multicollinearity among the IVs--independent variables--are unaffected by the DV).

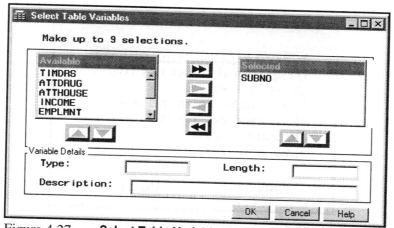

Figure 4.27   **Select Table Variables** list box for choosing
dummy DV.

Clicking on **OK** returns the **SAS/ASSIST Regression Analysis** dialog box of Figure 4.23, where clicking on the **Independent:** button again produces the **Select Table Variables** list. Figure 4.28 shows the selection of ATTDRUG, ATTHOUSE, MSTATUS, RACE, and LTIMEDRS as IVs.

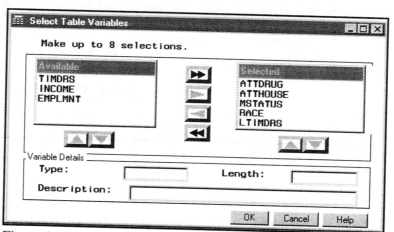

Figure 4.28   **Select Table Variables** dialog box for selecting
IVs.

Clicking on **OK** again returns the **SAS/ASSIST Regression Analysis** dialog box of Figure 4.23, where clicking on the **Additional Options** button produces the **Additional options** dialog box of Figure 4.29.

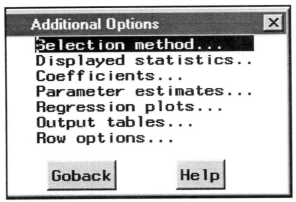

Figure 4.29   **Additional Options** menu.

Clicking on **Selection method...** produces the **Selection Method** dialog box of Figure 4.30, where choosing ⊙**RSQUARE** and then **OK** returns the **Additional Options** menu of Figure 4.29.

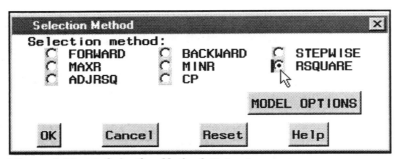

Figure 4.30   **Selection Method** dialog box.

Clicking on **Parameter estimates...** on the **Additional Options** menu produces the **Parameter Estimates** list, which allows you to choose **Collinearity analysis among independent columns** as seen in Figure 4.31. This produces the information for checking multicollinearity in Section 4.1.7 of this workbook. Clicking on **OK** returns the **Additional Options** menu.

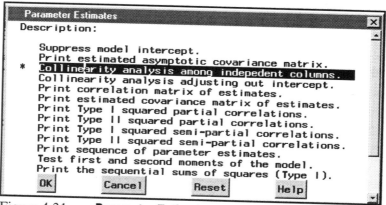

Figure 4.31   **Parameter Estimates** dialog box.

Clicking on **Output tables...** on the **Additional Options** menu produces the **Output tables** menu of Figure 4.32.

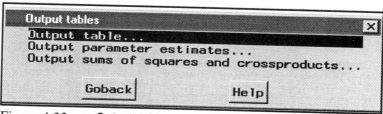

Figure 4.32   **Output tables** menu.

where clicking on **Output table...** produces the **Output Table** list of Figure 4.33

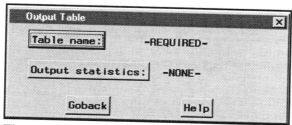

Figure 4.33   **Output Table** dialog box for choosing output data set name.

Clicking on the **Table name:** button produces a **Specify Output Table** dialog box in which SCREEN2 is typed in (Figure 4.34).

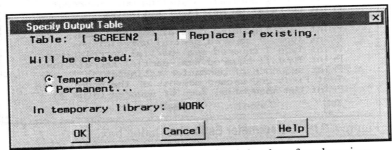

Figure 4.34   **Specify Output Table** dialog box for choosing data set name.

Note that the default ⊙**Temporary** output data set has been chosen; a permanent file may be specified in the **Specify Output Table** dialog box if desired. Clicking on OK returns the Output Table with the table name filled in (Figure 4.35).

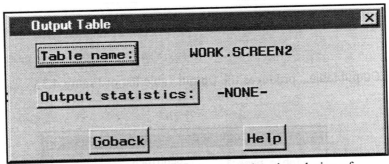

Figure 4.35   **Output Table** dialog box showing choice of WORK.SCREEN2.

Clicking on **Output statistics:** brings up the **Output Statistics** menu of Figure 4.36

40

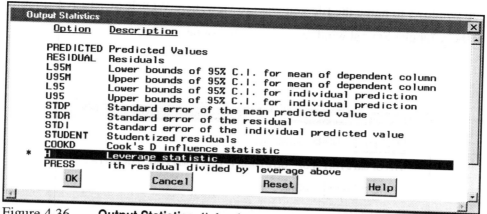

Figure 4.36   **Output Statistics** dialog box.

Note that Mahalanobis distance does not appear in this list. Instead **H** is selected (Leverage statistic). This can be converted to Mahalanobis distance by the following formula (Equation 4.3 in *Using Multivariate Statistics*):

$$mahalanobis \ distance \ = \ (N \ - \ 1)(h_{ii} \ - \ 1/N)$$

where h_{ii} is the leverage value (**H**) for the case.

Clicking on **OK** then allows you to click on **Goback** buttons of a few windows until you work your way back to the **SAS/ASSIST: Regression Analysis** dialog box, in which clicking the runner icon on the toolbar does the analysis and creates a data set that includes **H** values for each case. (Note that the only output of interest from the analysis contains the collinearity diagnostics to be discussed in Section 4.1.7 of this workbook. Output that is produced from this run is printed or saved by following directions for printing or saving an output file in Section 3.7.)

Working your way back to the main **SAS/ASSIST: WorkPlace** allows you to choose **Data Mgmt.** and view the new data file, SCREEN2, as per Section 3.3.1. Choose

> **E̲dit/Browse**
>> **B̲rowse data**
>>> **Browse data in tabular form**

41

This brings up windows to name the file you want to view, here WORK.SCREEN2. Figure 4.37 shows the **Browse Data in Tabular Format** window with the chosen table filled in.

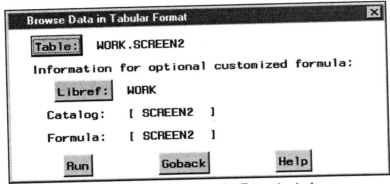

Figure 4.37   **Browse Data in Tabular Format** window.

Clicking on the runner icon produces the data set in the **FSVIEW: WORK.SCREEN2 (B)** window, displayed in Figure 4.38 where **H** is shown for several cases, including the 117th case.

Obs	RACE	LTIMDRS	OBSTAT				H
110	2	1.079181246	01101	0	0	0	0.0285824272
111	1	1.079181246	01101	0	0	0	0.0055887253
112	1	0.9542425094	01101	0	0	0	0.0053797113
113	1	0.4771212547	01101	0	0	0	0.0147160811
114	1	0.6989700043	01101	0	0	0	0.0066358771
115	1	0.6989700043	01101	0	0	0	0.0039127256
116	1	0.84509804	01101	0	0	0	0.0078068049
117	2	1.4913616938	01101	0	0	0	0.0494257157
118	1	0.903089987	01101	0	0	0	0.0120215171
119	1	1.2041199827	01101	0	0	0	0.0071757265
120	2	0.84509804	01101	0	0	0	0.0274051661
121	1	0.903089987	01101	0	0	0	0.0042049525
122	1	0.4771212547	01101	0	0	0	0.0072446448
123	1	0.3010299957	01101	0	0	0	0.0076947747
124	1	0.7781512504	01101	0	0	0	0.0044777477
125	1	0.3010299957	01101	0	0	0	0.0133424095
126	1	1.079181246	01101	0	0	0	0.0114632451
127	1	1.2304489214	01101	0	0	0	0.0159830102
128	1	0.4771212547	01101	0	0	0	0.0064790997
129	1	1.1760912591	01101	0	0	0	0.018264057
130	1	0.9542425094	01101	0	0	0	0.0053797113
131	1	1.255272505?	01101	0	0	0	0.012555595

Figure 4.38   **FSVIEW: WORK.SCREEN2(B)** window showing leverage values.

Applying Equation 4.3:

$$Mahalanobis\ distance\ =\ (463\ -\ 1)(0.0494257157\ -\ 1/463)\ =\ 21.83684$$

as per Table 4.8 in Using *Multivariate Statistics*.

4.1.7 Multicollinearity

Collinearity diagnostics were requested as part of the Linear Regression run in Section 4.1.6 that saved multivariate outlier statistics (see Figure 4.31). *Output 4.3* is produced after clicking on the runner icon from **SAS/ASSIST: Regression Analysis** with the request for collinearity diagnostics (before viewing the data set with leverage values).

Output 4.3 PARTIAL OUTPUT FROM LINEAR REGRESSION TO SHOW COLLINEARITY DIAGNOSTICS.

Collinearity Diagnostics

| | | | ----Proportion of Variation---- | | | |
Number	Intercept	ATTDRUG	ATTHOUSE	MSTATUS	RACE	LTIMDRS
1	0.00027053	0.00066855	0.00092595	0.00150	0.00186	0.00590
2	0.00092402	0.00167	0.00150	0.01114	0.01980	0.91802
3	0.00061052	0.00208	0.00589	0.28898	0.66215	0.01011
4	0.00400	0.03493	0.28983	0.45696	0.16056	0.06346
5	0.00416	0.53466	0.41480	0.06256	0.03940	0.00212
6	0.99003	0.42600	0.28707	0.17886	0.11622	0.00039485

4.1.8 Variables Causing Cases to be Outliers

The RSQUARE procedure used in Section 4.1.6 for identifying multivariate outliers and producing collinearity diagnostics is an all-subsets regression technique that produces minimal output. It is therefore not useful for identifying variables causing cases to be outliers. Thus the standard regression procedure will be used here as per Section 4.2.1.5 in *Using Multivariate Statistics*. You will need to close all data analysis windows before proceeding.

First, the dummy variable (to be used as the DV) is created using the **SAS/ASSIST: WorkPlace** by choosing

> **Solutions**
> > **ASSIST**
> > > **SAS/ASSIST: WorkPlace**
> > > > **Data Mgmt.**
> > > > > **Edit/Browse**
> > > > > > **Edit Data...**
> > > > > > **Tabular Format**

43

Edit Data in Tabular Format
Table: SCREEN1
Run

Clicking on **Run** produces the full screen editor, **FSVIEW: SASUSER.SCREEN1 (E)**. Chose **Tools** from the main menu strip, and then **Define formula**, which produces the **FSVIEW: Define command** dialog box of Figure 4.39.

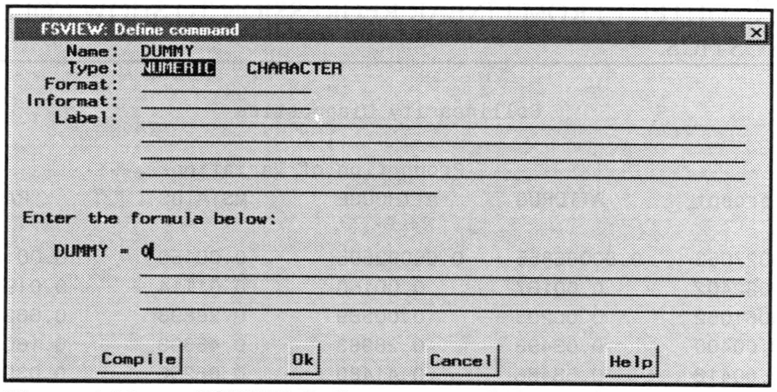

Figure 4.39 **FSVIEW: Define command** dialog box.

Typing in DUMMY for **Name:** (and pressing **Enter**) begins the equation by putting DUMMY on the left side of the formula. After the = sign, type in 0, then click on **OK**. This puts the new variable on screen, with DUMMY = 0 for all cases, however it cannot be modified to set DUMMY = 1 for the 117th case until a new data set is created.

Creating a new file involves choosing **File** from the main menu strip, then **Save as...** and which produces the **Save as** dialog box of Figure 4.40 for saving the file (named SASUSER.SCREEN3) with DUMMY in it.

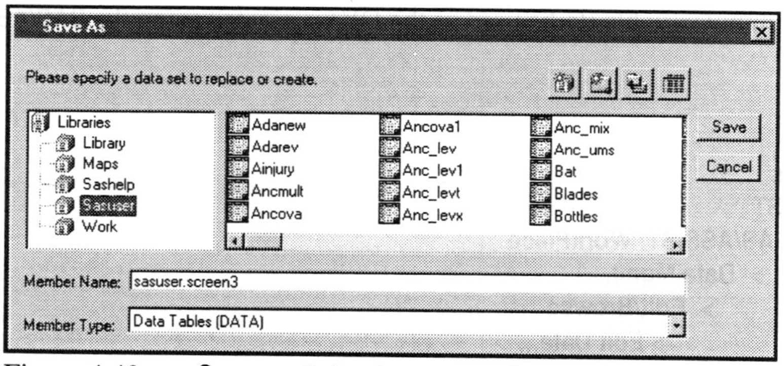

Figure 4.40 **Save as** dialog box.

Clicking on **OK** produces a window with a list of variables (not shown) with all of them selected by default. Clicking on **OK** creates the file **SASUSER.SCREEN3.**

Work your way back to the main SAS windows, and select

> **Solutions**
> > **Analysis**
> > > **Interactive Data Analysis**

as per Section 3.3.3. Select SASUSER.SCREEN3 as the data set in the **SAS/INSIGHT: Open** list (now shown, as per Figure 3.12).

Figure 4.41 shows the new data set. Scroll to the 117th case and the column with the DUMMY variable. Click on the cell, change the value from 0 to 1, and press **Enter**.

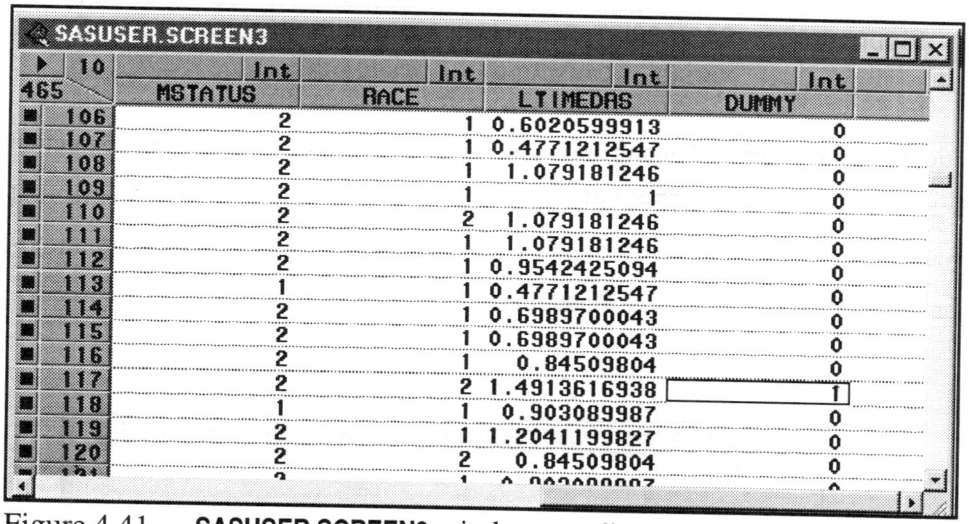

10	Int	Int	Int	Int
465	MSTATUS	RACE	LTIMEDRS	DUMMY
106	2	1	0.6020599913	0
107	2	1	0.4771212547	0
108	2	1	1.079181246	0
109	2	1	1	0
110	2	2	1.079181246	0
111	2	1	1.079181246	0
112	2	1	0.9542425094	0
113	1	1	0.4771212547	0
114	2	1	0.6989700043	0
115	2	1	0.6989700043	0
116	2	1	0.84509804	0
117	2	2	1.4913616938	1
118	1	1	0.903089987	0
119	2	1	1.2041199827	0
120	2	2	0.84509804	0

Figure 4.41   **SASUSER.SCREEN3** window to edit DUMMY for case #117.

This modified file now is saved as SASUSER.SCREEN4 by choosing

> **File**
> > **Save**
> > > **Data...**

from the main menu.

Stepwise regression is accessed through **SAS/ASSIST: WorkPlace** (Figure 3.5) as per Section 4.1.6 using SCREEN4 as the data set.

Figure 4.42 shows the **SAS/ASSIST: Regression Analysis** dialog box after choosing DUMMY as the DV; ATTDRUG, ATTHOUSE, MSTATUS, RACE, and LTIMEDRS as the IVs, and subsetting the data by excluding the univariate outliers on ATTHOUSE as per Figures 4.24 through 4.26.

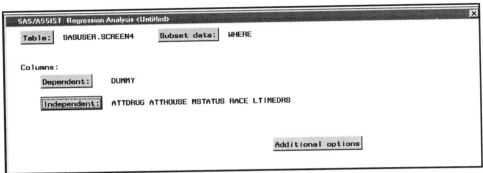

Figure 4.42   **SAS/ASSIST: Regression Analysis** dialog box for identifying variables causing multivariate outliers.

Clicking on **Additional Options** and then **Selection method...** produces the **Selection Method** dialog box of Figure 4.30, in which ⊙STEPWISE is selected. (There is no option in SAS ASSIST to select standard multiple regression. Instead, stepwise is chosen, with all variables forced into the model.) Clicking on **Model Options** returns the **Model Selection Options** menu of Figure 4.43.

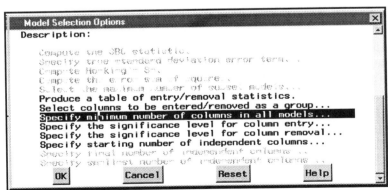

Figure 4.43   **Model Selection Options** menu to specify minimum number of columns (variables).

After scrolling down the window to bring the desired choice into view, clicking on **Specify minimum number of columns in all models...** produces the **Specify a Numeric Value** dialog box of Figure 4.44, in which 5 (all variables) is filled in. Forcing all variables into all models creates standard multiple regression.

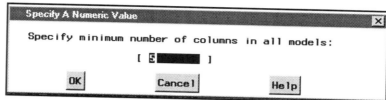

Figure 4.44   **Specify a Numeric Value** dialog box for selecting all 5 variables.

Clicking on **OK** a few times and **Goback** returns the **Regression Analysis** dialog box, where clicking on the runner icon produces *Output 4.4*.

Output 4.4 PARTIAL OUTPUT FROM STANDARD MULTIPLE REGRESSION TO IDENTIFY VARIABLES CAUSING CASE 177 TO BE AN OUTLIER.

Variable	Parameter Estimate	Standard Error	Type II SS	F Value	Pr > F
Intercept	-0.00503	0.02266	0.00010246	0.05	0.8245
* ATTDRUG	-0.00494	0.00184	0.01493	7.18	0.0076
* ATTHOUSE	0.00001630	0.00050537	0.00000216	0.00	0.9743
* MSTATUS	0.00397	0.00515	0.00123	0.59	0.4418
* RACE	0.02625	0.00749	0.02552	12.27	0.0005
* LTIMEDRS	0.01230	0.00520	0.01161	5.58	0.0185

Output matches that of Table 4.9 in *Using Multivariate Statistics*, with the exception that F is reported rather than t (recall that $F = t^2$).

4.2   SCREENING GROUPED DATA

The procedures for grouped data are similar to those of ungrouped data, with the major exception that analyses are done separately within each group.

4.2.1   Histograms and Descriptive Statistics

The **Interactive Data Analysis** procedures of Section 4.1 are followed (with SASUSER.SCREEN again selected as the data set) except that EMPLMNT is selected as a **Group** variable in the **Distribution(Y)** dialog box, as seen in Figure 4.45.

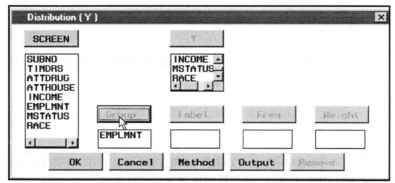

Figure 4.45   **Distribution(Y)** dialog box for screening data grouped by EMPLMNT.

Then procedures illustrated in Figure 4.5 are followed to produce the histograms and descriptive statistics. Results are shown for each group by scrolling horizontally and for each variable by scrolling vertically. Figure 4.46 shows the results for TIMEDRS for paid workers (EMPLMNT = 0) and Figure 4.47 shows the results for housewives (EMPLMNT = 1).

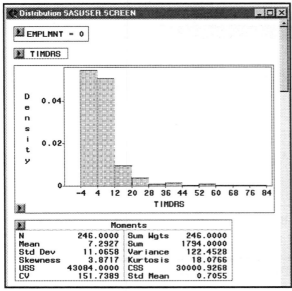

Figure 4.46   TIMEDRS histogram and
                descriptive statistics for paid
                workers.

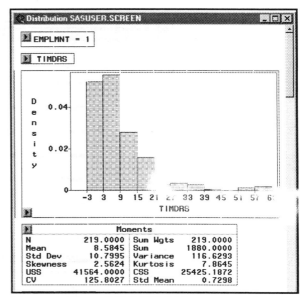

Figure 4.47   TIMEDRS histogram and
                descriptive statistics for
                housewives.

4.2.2   Scatterplots for Linearity

Again, the procedures for producing scatterplots for grouped data are the same as for ungrouped data
(Section 4.1.4) once the **Group** variable is specified. Figures 4.48 and 4.49 show the ATTDRUG by
TIMEDRS scatterplots for the two employment groups.

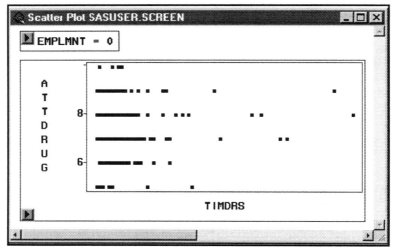

Figure 4.48   Scatterplot of ATTDRUG vs. TIMEDRS for paid workers.

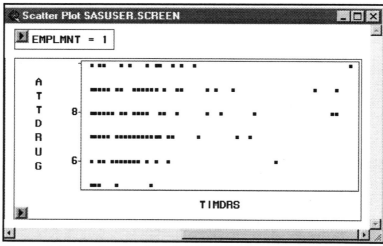

Figure 4.49   Scatterplot of ATTDRUG vs. TIMEDRS for housewives.

4.2.3   Multivariate Outliers and Multicollinearity

SAS for Windows has a provision for doing multiple regression by subsets (e.g., groups). Therefore the procedures of Section 4.1.6 can be followed with subsets stipulated, after omitting univariate outliers on ATTHOUSE. Figure 4.50 shows the **SAS/ASSIST: Regression Analysis** dialog box set up with DV and IVs. Additional options are selected as per Figures 4.24 through 4.36.

50

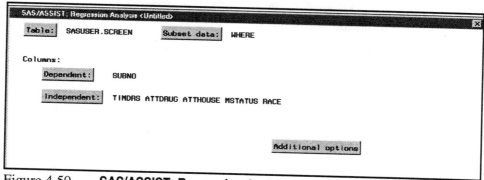

Figure 4.50   **SAS/ASSIST: Regression Analysis** dialog box for grouped data.

Click on the **Subset data:** button. This produces the **Subset Data** dialog box of Figure 4.51, where clicking on the **BY columns:** button brings up the **Select BY Columns** dialog box of Figure 4.52.

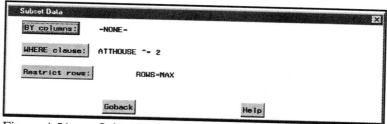

Figure 4.51   **Select Data** dialog box for grouped data.

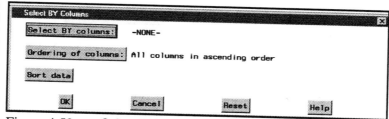

Figure 4.52   **Select BY Columns** dialog box.

Clicking on the **Select BY variables:** button produces the **Variables** list box of Figure 4.53, where EMPLMNT is selected.

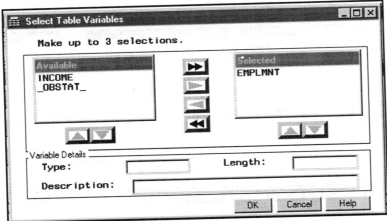

Figure 4.53   **Select Table Variables** list box for selecting
EMPLMNT as the grouping variable.

After clicking on **OK** to return the **Select BY columns** dialog box of 4.52, data must be sorted by the
grouping variable. This is done by clicking on the **Sort data** button, which produces a **SAS/ASSIST: Sort a
Table** dialog box (Figure 4.54).

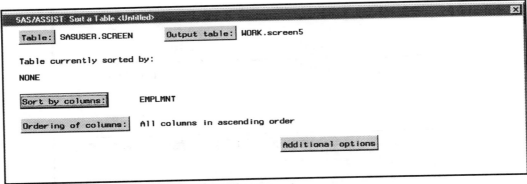

Figure 4.54   **SAS/ASSIST: Sort a Table** dialog box.

Clicking on the **Sort by columns:** button produces the **Select Table Variables** list from which to choose
EMPLMNT. You may also choose a new data set name (so you do not sort your original data set) by
clicking on the **Output table:** button, which produces the **Specify Output Table** dialog box in which to
choose SCREEN5 as a temporary data set. Clicking on **OK** returns the **Sort a Table** dialog box. The usual

52

run procedures are used to sort the data, after which a window shows that the data have been sorted in WORK.SCREEN5.

After working your way back to the **SAS/ASSIST Regression Analysis** dialog box, clicking on runner icon produces the analysis with multicollinearity statistics as well as a new data set that includes within-group **H** values as per those shown in Section 4.1.6. Applying Equation 4.3 to these values results in Mahalanobis distances that match those shown on Table 4.14 of *Using Multivariate Statistics*. Note that case numbers differ from those in Table 4.14 because data have been sorted by EMPLMNT.

Transformation of TIMEDRS (Section 4.1.5) proceeds as with ungrouped data. Identification of variables causing multivariate outliers through stepwise regression (cf. Section 4.1.8) by EMPLMNT groups follows, with TIMEDRS replaced by LTIMEDRS. This is best done by running separate regressions for the group containing the outlier, rather than using the BY procedure used for finding multivariate outliers. (At least one group will have no variability in the DV-- DUMMY -- since the search is done one case at a time.) The **WHERE clause** procedure (shown in Figures 4.25 and 4.26) is used to include only the group containing the outlier. Figure 4.55 shows the **Build A WHERE Clause to Subset the Current Data** dialog box to include housewives only. Be sure that the data set you use for this procedure is sorted by SUBNO, otherwise the case numbers for editing the DUMMY variable will not match those in *Using Multivariate Statistics*.

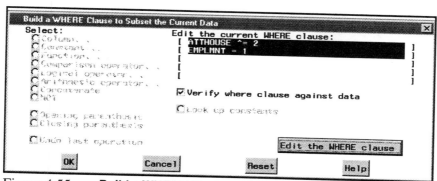

Figure 4.55   **Build a WHERE Clause to Subset the Current Data** dialog box to restrict analysis to housewives.

Multicollinearity output is produced by a regression run similar to the one that provides **H** values, except that the subsetting by group is turned off.

Chapter 5. Multiple Regression

This chapter demonstrates standard and sequential multiple regression, after evaluating assumptions for regression, using SAS/ASSIST in SAS for Windows for the complete examples of Chapter 5, *Using Multivariate Statistics*. The SAS data file to use is REGRESS.SAS7BDAT.

The first example evaluates prediction of visits to health professionals by physical and mental health symptoms and stress associated with major life changes in a standard multiple regression. The second example takes a sequential approach with the same predictors--first evaluating prediction of visits to health professionals (TIMEDRS) with physical health symptoms (PHYHEAL) alone, then evaluating gain in prediction with the addition of life change stress (STRESS), and finally evaluating additional gain in prediction with mental health symptoms (MENHEAL).

5.1 EVALUATION OF ASSUMPTIONS

Descriptive statistics, histograms, and transformations are demonstrated in Sections 4.1.1, 4.1.2, and 4.1.5 of this workbook. Detection of outliers through Mahalanobis distance using multiple regression is demonstrated in Section 4.1.6.

Multiple regression is used to produce a scatterplot of residuals. On the **SAS/ASSIST: WorkPlace** (Figures 3.4 and 3.5), click on **Data Analysis**, which produces a menu. Choosing

> **> Regression**
> **> Linear...**

produces the **SAS/ASSIST: Regression Analysis** dialog box of Figure 5.1.

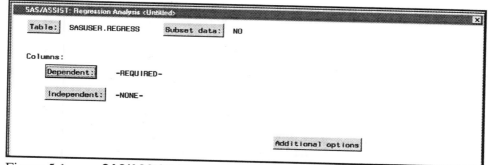

Figure 5.1   **SAS/ASSIST: Regression Analysis** dialog box for residuals scatterplots.

Clicking on **Dependent:** brings up the **Select Table Variables** list box, which allows you to choose TIMEDRS as the DV, as seen in Figure 5.2.

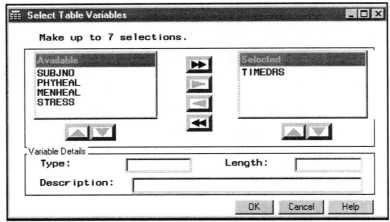

Figure 5.2   **Select Table Variables** list box for choosing
TIMEDRS as the DV.

Clicking on **OK** returns the **Regression Analysis** dialog box of Figure 5.1, where clicking on **Independent:** produces another **Select Table Variables** list box for choosing PHYHEAL, MENHEAL, and STRESS as the IVs, as seen in Figure 5.4.

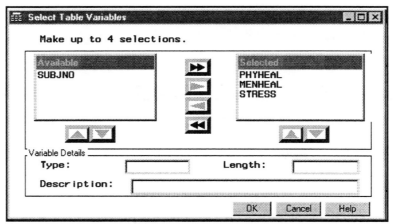

Figure 5.3   **Select Table Variables** list box for choosing IVs
for residuals scatterplot.

Clicking on **OK** returns the **Regression Analysis** dialog box, where clicking on **Additional options** produces the **Additional Options** dialog box of Figure 5.4.

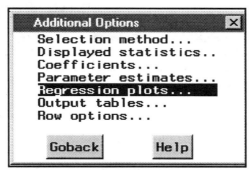

Figure 5.4   **Additional Options** dialog box for residuals scatterplots.

Clicking on **Regression plots...** produces the **Regression Plots** menu, where **Plot of studentized residuals by predicted values** is selected, as seen in Figure 5.5. (Plots with standardized predicted values are not directly available in SAS for Windows.)

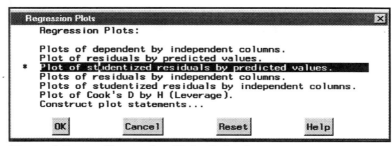

Figure 5.5   **Regression Plots** dialog box.

Clicking on **OK** returns the **Additional Options** menu of Figure 5.4, where choosing **Selection method...** produces the **Selection Method** dialog box of Figure 5.6 where ⊙ **RSQUARE**, which produces minimal regression output, is selected.

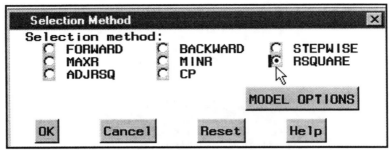

Figure 5.6   **Selection Method** dialog box for residuals
scatterplot.

Click on **OK** to return the **Additional Options** menu, where clicking on **Goback** returns the **Regression Analysis** dialog box of Figure 5.1. Clicking the runner icon produces Figure 5.7.

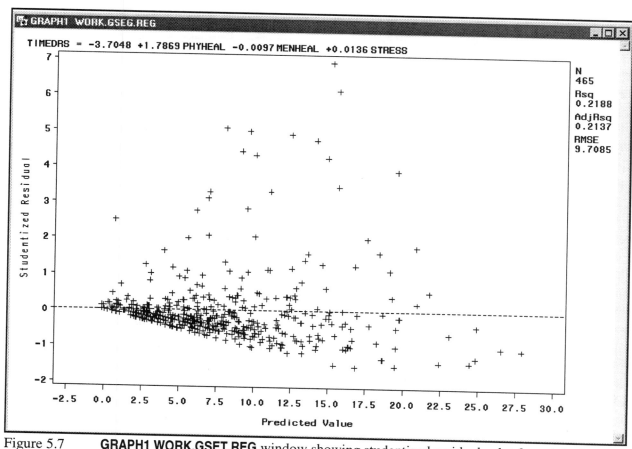

Figure 5.7   **GRAPH1 WORK.GSET.REG** window showing studentized residuals plot for original
variables.

The scatterplot shows the need for transformation of one or more variables. Transformation of STRESS
is accomplished by returning to the main SAS window and accessing **Interactive Data Processing** (as per
Section 3.3.3) and choosing the REGRESS file (as per Figure 3.12). This produces a window that shows
the data set. Choosing

> **Edit**
 > **Variables**
  > **sqrt(Y)**

produces the **Edit Variables** dialog box of Figure 5.8.

59

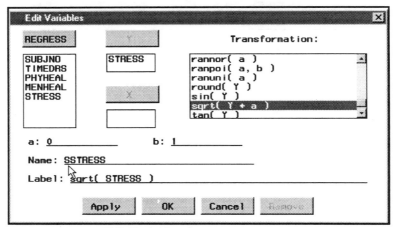

Figure 5.8   **Edit Variables** dialog box for creating SSTRESS.

Choose STRESS as the **Y** variable, and **sqrt(Y + a)** as the **Transformation:**. Also, the **Name:** may be edited to SSTRESS to match variables names in *Using Multivariate Statistics (UMS)*. Clicking on **OK** adds SSTRESS to the data set. Transformation of LTIMEDRS follows the procedures of Section 4.1.5, as does transformation of LPHYHEAL (which does not require the addition of 1 to each value before transformation, i.e., **a:** may be left at 0). Figure 5.9 shows a portion of the data set with the additional variables. The data set with transformed variables may be saved following procedures at the end of Section 4.1.5. Here the new data set is named REGRESS1.

8	Int MENHEAL	Int STRESS	Int LTIMEDRS	Int LPHYHEAL	Int SSTRESS		
465							
1	8	265	0.3010	0.6990	16.2788		
2	6	415	0.6021	0.6021	20.3715		
3	4	92	0.0000	0.4771	9.5917		
4	2	241	1.1461	0.3010	15.5242		
5	6	86	1.2041	0.4771	9.2736		
6	5	247	0.6021	0.6990	15.7162		
7	6	13	0.4771	0.6990	3.6056		
8	5	12	0.0000	0.6021	3.4641		
9	4	269	0.9031	0.6990	16.4012		
10	9	391	0.6990	0.4771	19.7737		
11	3	237	1.2041	0.7782	15.3948		
12	5	13	0.0000	0.4771	3.6056		
13	10	84	0.4771	0.4771	9.1652		
14	9	144	1.1461	0.7782	12.0000		
15	2	135	0.4771	0.4771	11.6190		

Figure 5.9   REGRESS data set showing transformed variables.

Multiple regression now can be rerun with the transformed variables. Requesting plots in the **Regression Analysis** dialog box and menus is identical to procedures illustrated in Figures 5.1 to 5.6, except that variables chosen for analysis are as in Figure 5.10.

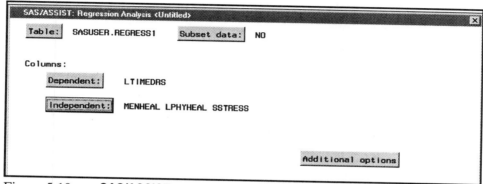

Figure 5.10   **SAS/ASSIST: Regression Analysis** dialog box for residuals scatterplot for transformed variables.

Clicking on the runner icon produces Figure 5.11. (Multicollinearity information is available in the main analysis that follows.)

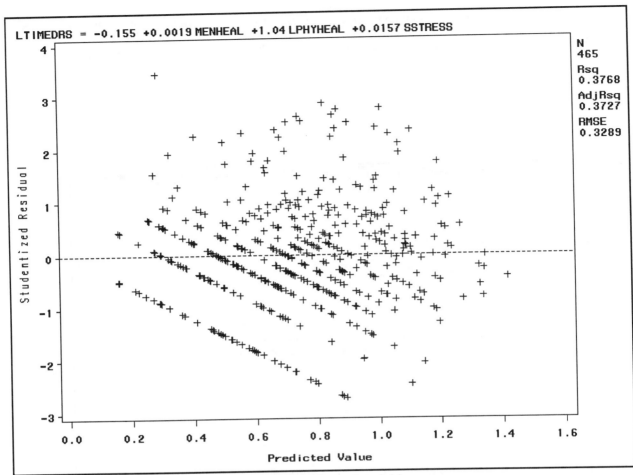

LTIMEDRS = -0.155 +0.0019 MENHEAL +1.04 LPHYHEAL +0.0157 SSTRESS

N
465
Rsq
0.3768
AdjRsq
0.3727
RMSE
0.3289

Figure 5.11   Studentized residuals plot for transformed variables.

5.2   STANDARD MULTIPLE REGRESSION

The choice of dependent and independent variables is as illustrated in Figure 5.10. Clicking on the **Additional Options:** button produces the **Additional Options** menu where you do three things. First, you may cancel the request for the regression plots to avoid excessive output. Second, choose **Selection method...** to produce the **Selection Method** dialog box, where **Forward** is chosen (Figure 5.12), and then **Model Options**, which produces the **Model Selection Options** menu of Figure 5.13.

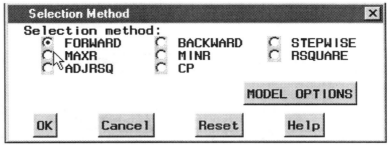

Figure 5.12   **Selection Method** dialog box for choosing
                FORWARD regression.

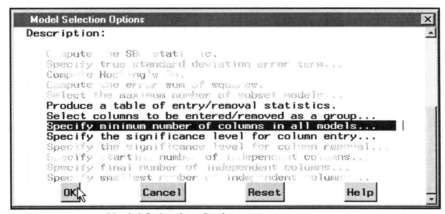

Figure 5.13   **Model Selection Options** dialog box.

Clicking on **Specify minimum number of columns in all models...** (you need to scroll down the list to get to this) brings up a box that allows you to specify 3 variables. This forces all three IVs into the regression equation Clicking on **OK** a few times for successive windows brings back the **Additional Options** menu.

　　　Third, choosing **Parameter estimates...** produces the **Parameter Estimates** dialog box, permitting you to select **Collinearity analysis among independent variables** and **Print Type II squared semi-partial correlations**, as seen in Figure 5.14.

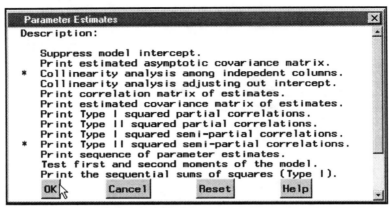

Figure 5.14   **Parameter Estimates** dialog box for collinearity analysis and sr_i^2.

Clicking on **OK,** then **Goback** returns the main **Regression Analysis** dialog box, where clicking on the runner icon produces *Output 5.1*.

Output 5.1 STANDARD MULTIPLE REGRESSION ANALYSIS OF LTIMEDRS (THE DV) WITH MENHEAL, SSTRESS, AND LPHYHEAL (THE IVs). PARTIAL OUTPUT.

```
                        The REG Procedure
                         Model: MODEL1
           Dependent Variable: LTIMEDRS log10( TIMEDRS + 1 )


                        Analysis of Variance

                              Sum of          Mean
Source                DF      Squares        Square     F Value    Pr > F

Model                  3     30.14607      10.04869       92.90    <.0001
Error                461     49.86410       0.10817
Corrected Total      464     80.01017


              Root MSE            0.32888   R-Square     0.3768
              Dependent Mean      0.74129   Adj R-Sq     0.3727
              Coeff Var          44.36682
```

Parameter Estimates

Variable	Label	DF	Parameter Estimate	Standard Error	t Value	Pr > |t|	Squared Semi-partial Corr Type II
Intercept	Intercept	1	-0.15504	0.05826	-2.66	0.0081	.
MENHEAL		1	0.00188	0.00440	0.43	0.6689	0.00024759
LPHYHEAL	log10(PHYHEAL)	1	1.03997	0.08718	11.93	<.0001	0.19236
SSTRESS	sqrt(STRESS)	1	0.01571	0.00336	4.67	<.0001	0.02949

Collinearity Diagnostics

Number	Eigenvalue	Condition Index	--------------Proportion of Variation--------------			
			Intercept	MENHEAL	LPHYHEAL	SSTRESS
1	3.68482	1.00000	0.00474	0.01368	0.00466	0.00695
2	0.20057	4.28618	0.06200	0.80047	0.00615	0.03216
3	0.07582	6.97148	0.06587	0.00073580	0.25220	0.84688
4	0.03879	9.74676	0.86739	0.18511	0.73699	0.11401

5.3   SEQUENTIAL REGRESSION

SAS for Windows has no procedure for sequential regression. The RSQUARE analysis produces all-subsets regression, which provides information that allows calculation of values such as change in R^2 and the significance of that change.

After filling in the **SAS/ASSIST: Regression Analysis** dialog box as per Figure 5.10, clicking on the **Additional options** button produces the **Additional Options** menu, where **Selection method...** is chosen. This produces the **Selection Method** dialog box (e.g., Figure 5.12) where ⊙**RSQUARE** is chosen. Clicking **OK** returns the **Additional Options** menu, where clicking on **Goback** returns the **Regression Analysis** dialog box.. Clicking the runner icon produces *Output 5.2*.

Output 5.2 ALL-SUBSETS REGRESSION TO PRODUCE VALUES FOR SEQUENTIAL
REGRESSION.

The REG Procedure
Model: MODEL1
R-Square Selection Method
Regression Models for Dependent Variable: LTIMEDRS

Number in Model	R-Square	Variables in Model
1	0.3431	LPHYHEAL
1	0.1289	SSTRESS
1	0.1261	MENHEAL
2	0.3765	LPHYHEAL SSTRESS
2	0.3473	MENHEAL LPHYHEAL
2	0.1844	MENHEAL SSTRESS
3	0.3768	MENHEAL LPHYHEAL SSTRESS

R-square (R^2) is provided for the first variable, LPHYHEAL, in the first line of models with a single variable: 0.3431. The first line of models with two variables provides R-square for the combination of LPHYHEAL and SSTRESS: 0.3765. Subtracting the former value from the latter shows the increase in R^2 (change in R-square) due to adding SSTRESS: .3765 - .3431 = .0334. Subtracting R^2 for the second step from R^2 for the model with all three variables shows the increase in R^2 due to adding MENHEAL: .3768 - .3765 = .0003.

The significance of adding variables at each step is assessed using Equation 5.13 of *UMS:*

$$F_{inc} = \frac{(R^2_{wi} - R^2_{wo})/M}{(1 - R^2_{wi})/df_{res}}$$

For example, at the second step, with $df_{res} = N - 2 - 1 = 462$,

$$F_{inc} = \frac{(.3765 - .3431)/1}{(1 - .3765)/462} = 24.75$$

This highly significant result is within rounding error of **F Change for Model 2** in Table 5.19 of *UMS.*

The SAS for Windows RSQUARE procedure does not produce a full table of the analysis at the last step. This, however, is available by running a standard multiple regression as demonstrated in Section 5.2 of this workbook.

Chapter 6. Canonical Correlation

This chapter demonstrates canonical correlation using SAS for Windows, for the complete example of Chapter 6, *Using Multivariate Statistics*. The SAS data set to use is CANON.SAS7BDAT.

This example examines relationships among a set of attitudinal and health variables. Attitudinal variables are attitudes toward the role of women (ATTROLE), locus of control (CONTROL), self esteem (ESTEEM) and attitudes toward current marital status (ATTMAR). Health variables are mental health symptoms (MENHEAL), physical health symptoms (PHYHEAL), visits to health professionals (TIMEDRS), attitude toward use of medication (ATTDRUG), and use of psychotropic drugs (DRUGUSE).

6.1   EVALUATION OF ASSUMPTIONS

The canonical analysis program in SAS for Windows has no provision for canonical variate plots. Therefore tests for normality, linearity, and homoscedasticity are done through SAS batch processing using CANCORR and PLOT as in Section 6.6.1.2 in *UMS*. Chapter 6 of *UMS* shows the need for log transforms of three of the health variables (TIMEDRS, PHYHEAL, and DRUGUSE) and one of the attitudinal variables (ATTMAR). Transformations to produce LTIMEDRS,, LPHYHEAL, LDRUGUSE, and LATTMAR are computed as per Section 4.1.5. (The SAS file, CANON.SAS7BDAT, includes these transformed variables.) Identification and interpretation of univariate and multivariate outliers is done separately for each set of variables, respectively, using the SAS STANDARD procedures of *UMS* Section 6.6.1.3 and multiple regression procedures of Section 4.1.6. Note that the six cases with data missing on locus of control or ATTMAR need to be deleted from both multiple regression runs to search for multivariate outliers. Section 4.2.3 shows how to omit cases in regression analysis.

No collinearity diagnostics are available through canonical analysis in SAS for Windows, nor are SMCs (squared multiple correlations) available through canonical analysis or the graphical interface for principal components analysis. However, as noted in *UMS* Section 6.6.1.4, protection against multicollinearity by SAS precludes concern unless there is some reason to expect very large SMCs within either set of variables.

6.2   CANONICAL CORRELATION

From the **SAS/ASSIST: WorkPlace** choose

>**Multivariate**
>>**Canonical correlation...**

This produces the **Canonical Correlation** dialog box of Figure 6.1 (with SASUSER.CANON selected as the **Table:**.) .

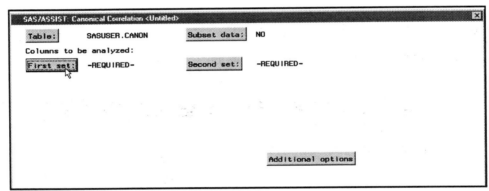

Figure 6.1   **SAS/ASSIST: Canonical Correlation** dialog box.

ESTEEM, CONTROL, ATTROLE, and LATTMAR are chosen as variables for the first set by clicking on **First set:**. This produces the **Select Table Variables** list box for choosing the first set of variables (Figure 6.2).

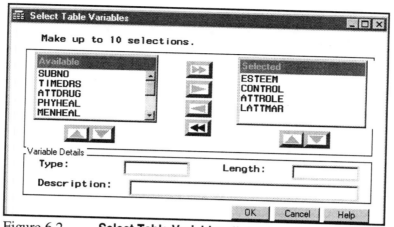

Figure 6.2   **Select Table Variables** dialog box for choosing
the first set of variables in canonical correlation.

After clicking on **OK**, the second set of canonical variables are chosen in similar fashion by clicking on
Second set: in the dialog box of Figure 6.1. The dialog box after choosing both sets of variables appears
in Figure 6.3.

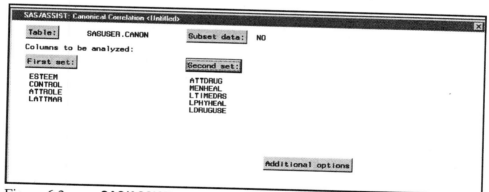

Figure 6.3   **SAS/ASSIST: Canonical Correlation** dialog box with variables
shown.

Clicking on **Additional options:** produces the **Additional Options** dialog box of Figure 6.4, in which
clicking on **Customize output...** produces the **Customized Output** dialog box of Figure 6.5.

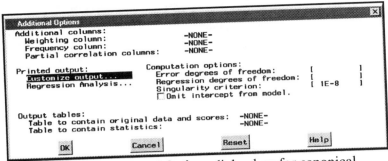

Figure 6.4   **Additional Options** dialog box for canonical correlation.

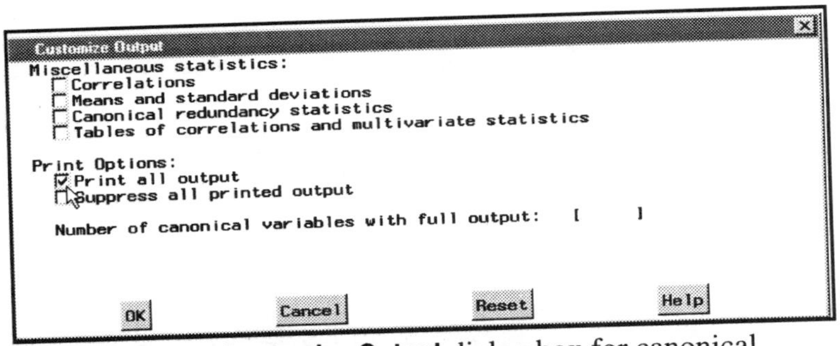

Figure 6.5   **Customize Output** dialog box for canonical correlation.

Here a request is made to **Print all output**. Clicking on **OK** returns the **Additional Options** dialog box, where clicking on **OK** returns the canonical correlation dialog box of Figure 6.3. Clicking on the runner icon produces output that is identical to that of Section 6.6.2 (Tables 6.12 to 6.15) in *UMS*.

Chapter 7. Multiway Frequency Analysis

This chapter demonstrates hierarchical loglinear analysis using SAS for Windows, for the complete example of Chapter 7, *Using Multivariate Statistics*. The SAS data set to use is MFA.SAS7BDAT.

This example demonstrates an evaluation of relationships among five dichotomous variables about reactions of clinical psychologists who were sexually attracted to their clients. Variables are whether the therapists thought (1) that their clients were aware of the therapist's attraction to them (AWARE), (2) the attraction was beneficial to the therapy (BENEFIT), and (3) the attraction was harmful to the therapy (HARM), as well as whether the therapist had (4) sought consultation when attracted to a client (CONSULT), or (5) felt uncomfortable as a result of the attraction (DISCOMF).

7.1 EVALUATION OF ASSUMPTIONS

Crosstabulation tables are used to evaluate adequacy of expected frequencies. Each 2 x 2 crosstab table is built individually, so that provision must be made to restrict all tables to cases with complete data.

SAS/ASSIST has difficulty with a restriction based on all five variables, so that a batch file is run to omit cases with incomplete data, with the restricted file saved as SASUSER.MFAC, as seen in Figure 7.1.

```
Program Editor - [Untitled]
data SASUSER.MFAC;
  set SASUSER.MFA;
if aware = . then delete;
if benefit = . then delete;
if harm = . then delete;
if consult = . then delete;
if discomf = . then delete;
run;
```

Figure 7.1   Batch file to create SASUSER.MFAC with complete cases.

Then, from **SAS/ASSIST WorkPlace**, choose

>Elementary
    >Frequency tables...
        >Generate N-Way Crosstabulation table...

This produces the **SAS/ASSIST: N-Way Frequency Table** dialog box of Figure 7.2.

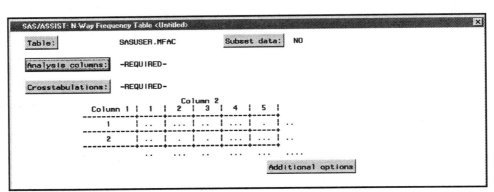

Figure 7.2   **SAS/ASSIST: N-Way Frequency Table** dialog box.

Note that **SASUSER.MFAC** has been selected as the **Table:**. Variables to be analyzed are selected by clicking on the **Analysis columns:** button, which produces the **Select Table Variables** dialog box of Figure 4.27. Only four variables at a time may be selected, so the variables selected are AWARE, BENEFIT, HARM, and CONSULT. Clicking on **OK** returns the main **N-Way Frequency Tables** dialog box, where tables are selected by clicking on the **Crosstabulations:** button. This produces the **Column Crosstabulations** menu to select the six two-way tables, as seen in Figure 7.3.

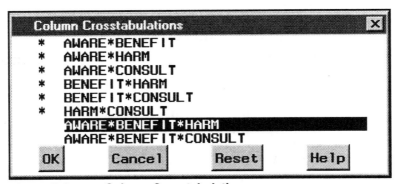

Figure 7.3   **Column Crosstabulations** menu.

Clicking on **OK** and then the runner icon produces *Output 7.1.*

TWO-WAY FREQUENCY TABLES FOR FOUR OF THE FIVE DICHOTOMOUS VARIABLES.

Table of AWARE by BENEFIT

```
AWARE(Client awareness)
            BENEFIT(Benefit to therapy)
 Frequency|
 Percent  |
 Row Pct  |
 Col Pct  |       1|       2|  Total
---------+--------+--------+
       1 |    129 |    177 |    306
         |  29.72 |  40.78 |  70.51
         |  42.16 |  57.84 |
         |  92.14 |  60.20 |
---------+--------+--------+
       2 |     11 |    117 |    128
         |   2.53 |  26.96 |  29.49
         |   8.59 |  91.41 |
         |   7.86 |  39.80 |
---------+--------+--------+
 Total        140      294      434
            32.26    67.74   100.00
```

Table of AWARE by HARM

```
AWARE(Client awareness)
            HARM(Harm to therapy)
 Frequency|
 Percent  |
 Row Pct  |
 Col Pct  |       1|       2|  Total
---------+--------+--------+
       1 |    173 |    133 |    306
         |  39.86 |  30.65 |  70.51
         |  56.54 |  43.46 |
         |  82.78 |  59.11 |
---------+--------+--------+
       2 |     36 |     92 |    128
         |   8.29 |  21.20 |  29.49
         |  28.13 |  71.88 |
         |  17.22 |  40.89 |
---------+--------+--------+
 Total        209      225      434
            48.16    51.84   100.00
```

73

Table of AWARE by CONSULT

AWARE(Client awareness)

CONSULT(Consultation sought)

Frequency Percent Row Pct Col Pct	1	2	Total
1	155 35.71 50.65 86.11	151 34.79 49.35 59.45	306 70.51
2	25 5.76 19.53 13.89	103 23.73 80.47 40.55	128 29.49
Total	180 41.47	254 58.53	434 100.00

Table of BENEFIT by HARM

BENEFIT(Benefit to therapy)

HARM(Harm to therapy)

Frequency Percent Row Pct Col Pct	1	2	Total
1	90 20.74 64.29 43.06	50 11.52 35.71 22.22	140 32.26
2	119 27.42 40.48 56.94	175 40.32 59.52 77.78	294 67.74
Total	209 48.16	225 51.84	434 100.00

74

```
                  Table of BENEFIT by CONSULT

BENEFIT(Benefit to therapy)
            CONSULT(Consultation sought)
Frequency|
Percent  |
Row Pct  |
Col Pct  |        1|        2|  Total
---------+--------+--------+
       1 |      85 |      55 |    140
         |   19.59 |   12.67 |  32.26
         |   60.71 |   39.29 |
         |   47.22 |   21.65 |
---------+--------+--------+
       2 |      95 |     199 |    294
         |   21.89 |   45.85 |  67.74
         |   32.31 |   67.69 |
         |   52.78 |   78.35 |
---------+--------+--------+
Total             180      254      434
               41.47    58.53   100.00



                   Table of HARM by CONSULT

HARM(Harm to therapy)
            CONSULT(Consultation sought)
Frequency|
Percent  |
Row Pct  |
Col Pct  |        1|        2|  Total
---------+--------+--------+
       1 |     114 |      95 |    209
         |   26.27 |   21.89 |  48.16
         |   54.55 |   45.45 |
         |   63.33 |   37.40 |
---------+--------+--------+
       2 |      66 |     159 |    225
         |   15.21 |   36.64 |  51.84
         |   29.33 |   70.67 |
         |   36.67 |   62.60 |
---------+--------+--------+
Total             180      254      434
               41.47    58.53   100.00
```

Two additional runs with the same subset restrictions are needed to produce the four remaining
frequency tables: one run with DISCOMF by three of the other four variables (AWARE, BENEFIT and
HARM) and a final run with DISCOMF by the remaining variable (CONSULT).

7.2   HIERARCHICAL LOGLINEAR ANALYSIS

SAS/ASSIST has no provision for multiway frequency analysis. Therefore, the analysis is done through batch processing (cf. Section 3.5).

Another complication in using SAS is that all zeroes are treated as structural zeroes (responses that could not possibly occur, like pregnant men) rather than random zeroes (responses that actually could occur but did not do so in the data). That is, all cells must have frequencies greater than zero. For this latter reason, a new data set is developed, called MFATAB.DAT. This file is in ASCII format, with one row for each cell. Cell frequency is the last variable. Frequencies of zero have been replaced by very small numbers: 1E-27.

A final complication is that a screening run with this data set cannot accommodate the full 5-way model (all chi-square values are zero). Nor are sensible results available by omitting the 5-way association and screening a model that includes all 4-way associations. The decision is made to evaluate a model that includes all 3-way associations. Figure 7.4 shows the batch file to produce that screening run, akin to Table 7.15 in *Using Multivariate Statistics.*

```
Program Editor - mfatab.sas  PROC CATMOD running
data SAMPLE;
infile 'A:\MFATAB.DAT';
input CONSULT DISCOMF AWARE HARM BENEFIT FREQ;
proc     catmod;
         weight FREQ;
         model CONSULT*DISCOMF*AWARE*HARM*BENEFIT=_RESPONSE_/
             pred=FREQ ML NOGLS;
         loglin CONSULT|DISCOMF|AWARE|HARM|BENEFIT@3;
run;
```

Figure 7.4   Batch file to produce screening run for hierarchical loglinear analysis.

Clicking on the runner icon submits the batch job, producing *Output 7.2.*

Output 7.2 PARTIAL OUTPUT FOR SCREENING FOR HIERARCHICAL LOGLINEAR ANALYSIS.

The CATMOD Procedure

Response   CONS*DISC*AWAR*HARM*BENE   Response Levels   32

```
Weight Variable    FREQ              Populations         1
Data Set           SAMPLE            Total Frequency   434
Frequency Missing  0                 Observations       32


                    Sample    Sample Size
                    --------------------
                       1          434


              Maximum Likelihood Analysis of Variance

        Source                 DF   Chi-Square    Pr > ChiSq
        --------------------------------------------------------
        CONSULT                 1       1.39        0.2377
        DISCOMF                 1      11.22        0.0008
        CONSULT*DISCOMF         1       6.43        0.0112
        AWARE                   1      37.00        <.0001
        CONSULT*AWARE           1       4.62        0.0316
        DISCOMF*AWARE           1       0.11        0.7383
        CONSULT*DISCOMF*AWARE   1       2.17        0.1403
        HARM                    1       1.41        0.2345
        CONSULT*HARM            1       3.81        0.0510
        DISCOMF*HARM            1      15.55        <.0001
        CONSULT*DISCOMF*HARM    1       0.06        0.8137
        AWARE*HARM              1       9.70        0.0018
        CONSULT*AWARE*HARM      1       0.62        0.4328
        DISCOMF*AWARE*HARM      1       0.74        0.3890
        BENEFIT                 1      28.69        <.0001
        CONSULT*BENEFIT         1       5.60        0.0179
        DISCOMF*BENEFIT         1       0.07        0.7917
        CONSULT*DISCOMF*BENEFIT 1       0.42        0.5147
        AWARE*BENEFIT           1      15.11        0.0001
        CONSULT*AWARE*BENEFIT   1       0.67        0.4117
        DISCOMF*AWARE*BENEFIT   1       0.15        0.6971
        HARM*BENEFIT            1       0.32        0.5731
        CONSULT*HARM*BENEFIT    1       0.41        0.5209
        DISCOMF*HARM*BENEFIT    1       1.05        0.3066
        AWARE*HARM*BENEFIT      1       4.12        0.0423

        Likelihood Ratio        6      10.16        0.1180
```

Note that the results differ considerably from those of the example in *UMS*, and are generally more conservative. On the basis of this analysis, stepwise modeling would include only six of the 2-way associations. Without tests of all effects at a given level of association, the 3-way association between AWARE, HARM, and BENEFIT would be considered. (Note that Table 7.15 in *UMS* also shows that association to be significant if considered by itself.) However, the decision is made not to include that association in stepwise modeling because of its marginal probability level (.0423) and the fact that it is the only 3-way association that approaches statistical reliability. Note also that the `Likelihood Ratio` for the model with all 3-way effects is adequate, with a probability level in excess of .05.

Output 7.2 thus shows that the first model to be examined is one that includes six of the 2-way associations. Figure 7.5 and *Output 7.3* show the syntax and results of such an analysis. Note that all first order effects also are included explicitly in this hierarchical model. SAS, a general loglinear modeling program, does not include component lower order effects automatically.

```
Program Editor - mfatab2.sas
data SAMPLE;
infile 'A:\MFATAB.DAT';
input CONSULT DISCOMF AWARE HARM BENEFIT FREQ;
proc    catmod;
        weight FREQ;
        model CONSULT*DISCOMF*AWARE*HARM*BENEFIT=_RESPONSE_/
            pred=FREQ ML NOGLS;
        loglin CONSULT DISCOMF AWARE HARM BENEFIT
                CONSULT*DISCOMF CONSULT*AWARE DISCOMF*HARM
                AWARE*HARM CONSULT*BENEFIT AWARE*BENEFIT;
run;
```

Figure 7.5   Batch file for model based on screening run.

Output 7.3 PARTIAL OUTPUT FOR HIERARCHICAL MODEL BASED ON SCREENING RUN IN OUTPUT 7.2.

Maximum Likelihood Analysis of Variance

Source	DF	Chi-Square	Pr > ChiSq
CONSULT	1	4.72	0.0297
DISCOMF	1	29.00	<.0001
AWARE	1	81.62	<.0001
HARM	1	0.81	0.3670
BENEFIT	1	53.63	<.0001
CONSULT*DISCOMF	1	32.11	<.0001
CONSULT*AWARE	1	16.98	<.0001
DISCOMF*HARM	1	37.71	<.0001
AWARE*HARM	1	22.93	<.0001
CONSULT*BENEFIT	1	14.90	0.0001
AWARE*BENEFIT	1	28.17	<.0001
Likelihood Ratio	20	36.70	0.0127

Note that with a likelihood ratio $\chi^2(20) = 36.70$, $p < .05$, this is a poorly fitting model. Therefore, the decision is made to test a model that includes all 2-way associations, with the hope that an adequate model may be found that requires no higher order effects. Syntax and results of this model are seen in Figure 7.6 and *Output 7.4.*

```
data SAMPLE;
infile 'A:\MFATAB.DAT';
input CONSULT DISCOMF AWARE HARM BENEFIT FREQ;
proc    catmod;
        weight FREQ;
        model CONSULT*DISCOMF*AWARE*HARM*BENEFIT=_RESPONSE_/
          pred=FREQ ML NOGLS;
        loglin CONSULT|DISCOMF|AWARE|HARM|BENEFIT@2;
run;
```

Figure 7.6   Hierarchical model with all second-order effects.

Output 7.4 PARTIAL OUTPUT FOR HIERARCHICAL MODEL WITH ALL 2-WAY EFFECTS.

Maximum Likelihood Analysis of Variance

Source	DF	Chi-Square	Pr > ChiSq
CONSULT	1	5.71	0.0169
DISCOMF	1	16.28	<.0001
CONSULT*DISCOMF	1	21.08	<.0001
AWARE	1	74.13	<.0001
CONSULT*AWARE	1	14.89	0.0001
DISCOMF*AWARE	1	0.26	0.6080
HARM	1	0.17	0.6801
CONSULT*HARM	1	4.31	0.0378
DISCOMF*HARM	1	27.83	<.0001
AWARE*HARM	1	11.34	0.0008
BENEFIT	1	49.69	<.0001
CONSULT*BENEFIT	1	9.72	0.0018
DISCOMF*BENEFIT	1	0.31	0.5753
AWARE*BENEFIT	1	24.57	<.0001
HARM*BENEFIT	1	4.68	0.0306
Likelihood Ratio	16	24.09	0.0876

This output shows a model with adequate fit, but suggests that two of the second-order associations are unnecessary to the model: DISCOMF by AWARE and DISCOMF by BENEFIT.

Setup and results for a reduced model with all 1-way effects and eight of the 2-way effects are shown in Figure 7.7 and *Output 7.5.*

```
data SAMPLE;
infile 'A:\MFATAB.DAT';
input CONSULT DISCOMF AWARE HARM BENEFIT FREQ;
proc    catmod;
        weight FREQ;
        model CONSULT*DISCOMF*AWARE*HARM*BENEFIT=_RESPONSE_/
            pred=FREQ ML NOGLS;
        loglin CONSULT DISCOMF AWARE HARM BENEFIT
               CONSULT*AWARE DISCOMF*HARM
               AWARE*HARM AWARE*BENEFIT HARM*BENEFIT
               CONSULT*DISCOMF CONSULT*HARM CONSULT*BENEFIT;
run;
```

Figure 7.7   Hierarchical loglinear model with eight 2-way effects.

Output 7.5 PARTIAL OUTPUT FOR HIERARCHICAL MODEL WITH EIGHT 2-WAY
EFFECTS.

The CATMOD Procedure

Response	CONS*DISC*AWAR*HARM*BENE	Response Levels	32
Weight Variable	FREQ	Populations	1
Data Set	SAMPLE	Total Frequency	434
Frequency Missing	0	Observations	32

Sample	Sample Size
1	434

Response Profiles

Response	CONSULT	DISCOMF	AWARE	HARM	BENEFIT
1	1	1	1	1	1
2	1	1	1	1	2
3	1	1	1	2	1
4	1	1	1	2	2
5	1	1	2	1	1
6	1	1	2	1	2
7	1	1	2	2	1
8	1	1	2	2	2
9	1	2	1	1	1
10	1	2	1	1	2
11	1	2	1	2	1
12	1	2	1	2	2
13	1	2	2	1	1
14	1	2	2	1	2
15	1	2	2	2	1
16	1	2	2	2	2
17	2	1	1	1	1
18	2	1	1	1	2
19	2	1	1	2	1

80

20	2	1	1	2	2
21	2	1	2	1	1
22	2	1	2	1	2
23	2	1	2	2	1
24	2	1	2	2	2
25	2	2	1	1	1
26	2	2	1	1	2
27	2	2	1	2	1
28	2	2	1	2	2
29	2	2	2	1	1
30	2	2	2	1	2
31	2	2	2	2	1
32	2	2	2	2	2

Maximum Likelihood Analysis of Variance

Source	DF	Chi-Square	Pr > ChiSq
CONSULT	1	5.38	0.0204
DISCOMF	1	29.64	<.0001
AWARE	1	77.70	<.0001
HARM	1	0.26	0.6119
BENEFIT	1	52.25	<.0001
CONSULT*AWARE	1	14.78	0.0001
DISCOMF*HARM	1	29.31	<.0001
AWARE*HARM	1	11.26	0.0008
AWARE*BENEFIT	1	24.47	<.0001
HARM*BENEFIT	1	5.74	0.0166
CONSULT*DISCOMF	1	23.15	<.0001
CONSULT*HARM	1	4.39	0.0361
CONSULT*BENEFIT	1	11.19	0.0008
Likelihood Ratio	18	24.55	0.1379

Analysis of Maximum Likelihood Estimates

Effect	Parameter	Estimate	Standard Error	Chi-Square	Pr > ChiSq
CONSULT	1	-0.1663	0.0717	5.38	0.0204
DISCOMF	2	-0.3018	0.0554	29.64	<.0001
AWARE	3	0.7936	0.0900	77.70	<.0001
HARM	4	0.0351	0.0692	0.26	0.6119
BENEFIT	5	-0.6171	0.0854	52.25	<.0001
CONSULT*AWARE	6	0.2563	0.0667	14.78	0.0001
DISCOMF*HARM	7	0.3022	0.0558	29.31	<.0001
AWARE*HARM	8	0.2056	0.0558	11.26	0.0008
AWARE*BENEFIT	9	0.4276	0.0864	24.47	<.0001
HARM*BENEFIT	10	0.1381	0.0577	5.74	0.0166
CONSULT*DISCOMF	11	0.2650	0.0551	23.15	<.0001
CONSULT*HARM	12	0.1183	0.0564	4.39	0.0361
CONSULT*BENEFIT	13	0.1915	0.0572	11.19	0.0008

The CATMOD Procedure

Maximum Likelihood Predicted Values for Response Functions and Frequencies

81

Sample	CONSULT	DISCOMF	AWARE	HARM	BENEFIT	Function Number	Observed Function	Standard Error
1						1	-0.2818512	0.20198929
						2	-0.7472144	0.23362555
						3	-2.6567569	0.51724642
						4	-1.645156	0.32932196
						5	-66.212849	3.16228E13
						6	-2.944439	0.59234888
						7	-4.0430513	1.00873379
						8	-2.4336134	0.46641597
						9	-1.047319	0.25989202
						10	-1.4039939	0.29828247
						11	-1.4039939	0.29828247
						12	-0.9520088	0.25099483
						13	-66.212849	3.16228E13
						14	-2.0971411	0.40050094
						15	-2.944439	0.59234888
						16	-2.2512918	0.42919754
						17	-1.7404662	0.3428467
						18	-1.4781019	0.30735474
						19	-2.6567569	0.51724642
						20	-2.0971411	0.40050094
						21	-4.0430513	1.00873379
						22	-1.7404662	0.3428467
						23	-66.212849	3.16228E13
						24	-1.4039939	0.29828247
						25	-1.2704625	0.28292024
						26	-0.6418539	0.22555973
						27	-1.1526795	0.27036904
						28	-0.0727594	0.19081872
						29	-66.212849	3.16228E13
						30	-1.3350011	0.2901905
						31	-2.2512918	0.42919754
	1	1	1	1	1	F1	43	6.22411691
	1	1	1	1	2	F2	27	5.03192572
	1	1	1	2	1	F3	4	1.99076208
	1	1	1	2	2	F4	11	3.27432408
	1	1	2	1	1	F5	1E-27	3.1623E-14
	1	1	2	1	2	F6	3	1.72605408
	1	1	2	2	1	F7	1	0.99884726
	1	1	2	2	2	F8	5	2.22315009
	1	2	1	1	1	F9	20	4.36787603
	1	2	1	1	2	F10	14	3.68081337
	1	2	1	2	1	F11	14	3.68081337
	1	2	1	2	2	F12	22	4.56998825

82

Sample	CONSULT	DISCOMF	AWARE	HARM	BENEFIT	Function Number	Predicted Function	Standard Error	Residual
1						1	-0.512898	0.1740016	0.23104688
						2	-0.7930939	0.188818	0.04587953
						3	-2.111573	0.26931922	-0.5451839
						4	-1.8393451	0.25553204	0.19418914
						5	-3.8789387	0.42981141	-62.33391
						6	-2.4489225	0.30193014	-0.4955165
						7	-4.6552745	0.44408714	0.61222322
						8	-2.6728346	0.28681191	0.23922125
						9	-1.0436296	0.20243041	-0.0036894
						10	-1.3238255	0.21529922	-0.0801684
						11	-1.433353	0.2299336	0.0293591
						12	-1.1611252	0.21361939	0.2091164
						13	-4.4096703	0.44208524	-61.803179
						14	-2.9796541	0.31916034	0.88251297
						15	-3.9770546	0.42136683	1.0326156
						16	-1.9946147	0.2501953	-0.2566771
						17	-1.8424104	0.24610901	0.10194423
						18	-1.3565492	0.2248708	-0.1215527
						19	-2.967978	0.29150709	0.31122107
						20	-1.9296931	0.25094392	-0.167448
						21	-4.1833007	0.41690491	0.14024944
						22	-1.9872275	0.2437952	0.24676131
						23	-4.4865292	0.38767489	-61.72632
						24	-1.7380322	0.19293446	0.3340383
						25	-1.3133297	0.21954306	0.04286712
						26	-0.8274685	0.19543897	0.18561461
						27	-1.2299457	0.21852386	0.07726623
						28	-0.1916608	0.1604654	0.11890149
						29	-3.65422	0.401795	-62.558629
						30	-1.4581467	0.2169461	0.12314568
						31	-2.7484969	0.33625602	0.49720515
	1	1	1	1	1	F1	37.1066526	4.84055677	5.89334735
	1	1	1	1	2	F2	28.0391116	4.06986792	-1.0391116
	1	1	1	2	1	F3	7.50163763	1.69844849	-3.5016376
	1	1	1	2	2	F4	9.84879561	2.07711917	1.15120439
	1	1	2	1	1	F5	1.28114683	0.5007324	-1.2811468
	1	1	2	1	2	F6	5.35361375	1.40704583	-2.3536138
	1	1	2	2	1	F7	0.58944127	0.24626611	0.41055873
	1	1	2	2	2	F8	4.27960064	1.14249372	0.72039936
	1	2	1	1	1	F9	21.8251873	3.44652714	-1.8251873
	1	2	1	1	2	F10	16.4918908	2.80790868	-2.4918908
	1	2	1	2	1	F11	14.7809807	2.82834763	-0.7809807
	1	2	1	2	2	F12	19.4057437	3.35177762	2.59425625

This model fits well with no unnecessary effects. Further, it is not significantly worse than either of the more complete 2-way models, with χ^2 for difference less than 1.00 when compared with the model with ten 2-way effects or the model with nine 2-way effects. Thus, the resulting model is identical to the one found by stepwise model selection in Section 7.7.2.2 of *Using Multivariate Statistics*.

Output in the section labeled `Maximum-likelihood Predicted Values for Response Functions and Frequencies` provides residuals for each cell, as well as loglinear parameter estimates and their standard errors. Observed and expected frequencies also are provided.

The trick to identifying cells is in the response profiles at the beginning of the output. Response 1 is the cell that is labeled F1 near the end of the output. Therefore, the cell with negative responses to all items has an observed frequency of 43, an expected frequency of 37.1, for a residual of 5.89. Recall from Section 7.4.3.1 of *UMS* that a standardized residual is the residual divided by the square root of the expected frequency. So, for this cell,

$$z = \frac{5.8933}{\sqrt{37.107}} = 0.967$$

which compares with 1.0 in Table 7.17 of *UMS*.

Parameter estimates appear in the section of output Labeled `Analysis of Maximum-likelihood Estimates`. Note that these parameter estimates are identical to those in Table 7.18 of *UMS*. Dividing the parameter estimates by their standard errors produces the standardized loglinear parameter estimates. Signs for the parameter estimates correspond to the cells with the lower coded values. For example, the value of -.1663 for CONSULT corresponds for therapists responding NEVER to the item. The value of 0.265 for CONSULT by DISCOMF refers to therapists responding NEVER to both items.

Chapter 8. Analysis of Covariance

This chapter demonstrates analysis of covariance using SAS for Windows, for the complete example of Chapter 8, *Using Multivariate Statistics*. The data set to use is ANCOVA.SAS7BDAT.

This example evaluates whether attitudes toward medication are associated with current employment status (EMPLMNT) and/or religious affiliation (RELIGION), after statistically controlling for state of physical (PHYHEAL) and mental health (MENHEAL) and use of mood-modifying drugs (DRUGUSE).

8.1   EVALUATION OF ASSUMPTIONS

Frequencies and histograms are formed as illustrated in Section 4.2.1 of this workbook, noting that eight groups must be formed on the basis of two variables: RELIGION and EMPLMNT.

Figure 8.1 shows the **Distribution(Y)** dialog box with the request for two grouping variables (only one of which shows in the display) and four **Y** variables (only three of which show in the display). Recall that you may limit output to **Moments** and **Histogram/Bar Chart.** Results for PSYDRUG in the first group are in Figure 8.2. Additional results are found by scrolling. (Ignore results for groups in which RELIGION and/or EMPLMNT are missing.)

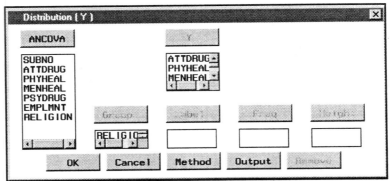

Figure 8.1   **Distribution(Y)** dialog box for analysis of covariance.

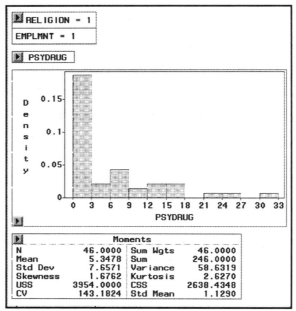

Figure 8.2   PSYDRUG histogram and
descriptive statistics for
employed women responding
none or other to religious
affiliation.

This provides screening for univariate outliers, sample sizes, normality, and homogeneity of variance. Linearity among covariates and between the DV and each covariate is evaluated by procedures discussed in Section 4.2.2. Multivariate outliers and evaluation of multicollinearity are found through multiple regression separately for each group, as discussed in Section 4.2.3.

These procedures highlight the need to apply a logarithmic transform (as demonstrated in Chapter 4) to PHYHEAL, producing LPHYHEAL; and to PSYDRUG, producing LPYSDRUG (note that 1 is to be added to PSYDRUG before log transform.) The data set with transformed variables is saved as SASUSER.ANCOVA1.

Homogeneity of regression is not tested automatically in any analysis of variance programs in SAS. However, it can be evaluated by forming interactions between effects (main effects and interactions) and covariates through the analysis of covariance procedure demonstrated in the next section. Although covariates cannot be pooled, each covariate can be evaluated separately. Thus, the tests for homogeneity of regression will be demonstrated in Section 8.2.2 after the main analysis of covariance.

8.2   ANALYSIS OF COVARIANCE

8.2.1   Major Analysis

Analysis of covariance is access from the **SAS/ASSIST: WorkPlace** by choosing

> **Data Analysis**
> > **Anova**
> > > **Analysis of Variance...**

This produces the **SAS/ASSIST: Analysis of Variance** dialog box of Figure 8.3.

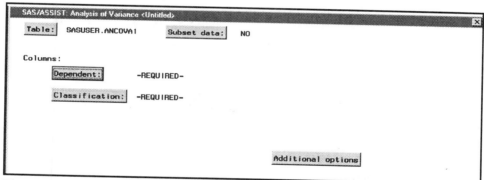

Figure 8.3   **SAS/ASSIST: Analysis of Variance** dialog box.

Clicking on the **Dependent:** box produces the **Select Table Variables** list box of Figure 8.4 in which ATTDRUG is chosen as the DV.

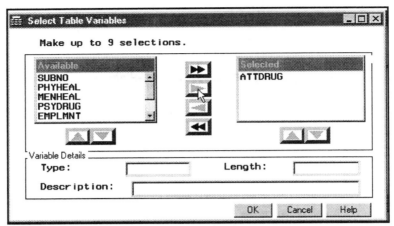

Figure 8.4   **Select Table Variables** list box for choosing the DV.

Clicking on **OK** returns the **Analysis of Variance** dialog box of Figure 8.3, where clicking on the **Classification:** button again produces the **Select Table Variables** list box for choosing the IVs. Note that the order of the choice is important in this sequential analysis. RELIGION must be chosen prior to EMPLMNT if it is to be the highest priority IV, as seen in Figure 8.5.

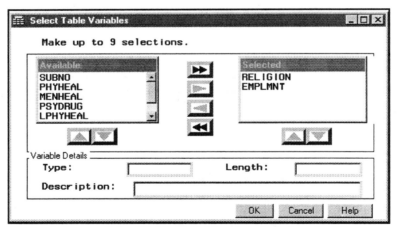

Figure 8.5   **Select Table Variables** for choosing the IVs.

Clicking on **OK** returns the **Analysis of Variance** dialog box again.

Clicking on **Additional options** produces the **Additional Options** menu of Figure 8.6.

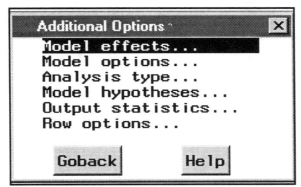

Figure 8.6   **Additional Options** menu for
             analysis of covariance.

Clicking on **Model effects...** produces the **Model Effects** menu of Figure 8.7.

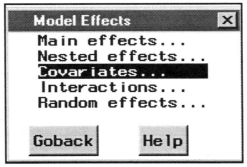

Figure 8.7   **Model Effects** dialog
             box.

Clicking in **Covariates...** produces the **Select Table Variables** list box of Figure 8.8, in which LPHYHEAL, MENHEAL, and LPSYDRUG are selected.

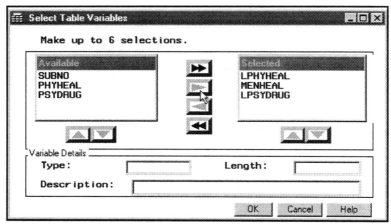

Figure 8.8   **Select Table Variables** list box for selecting covariates.

Clicking on **OK** returns the **Model Effects** menu of Figure 8.6, in which clicking on **Interactions...** produces the **Interactions** dialog box of Figure 8.9. Clicking on RELIGION, then |, and then EMPLMNT indicates that the two-way interaction is to be included in the model along with the two main effects. (Note that the main effects of RELIGION and EMPLMNT appear if you click on **Main effects...** on the **Model Effects** menu.)

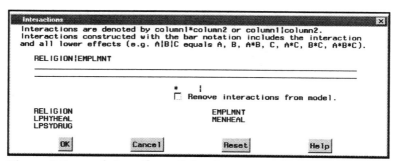

Figure 8.9   **Interactions** dialog box.

Clicking on **OK** and then **Goback** returns the **Additional Options** menu, where clicking on **Output statistics...** produces the **Output Statistics** menu of Figure 8.10.

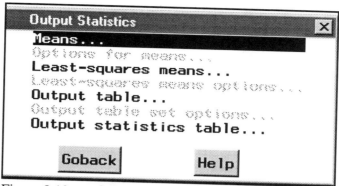

Figure 8.10   **Output Statistics** dialog box.

Clicking on **Means...** provides the **Effect Selection** menu of Figure 8.11.

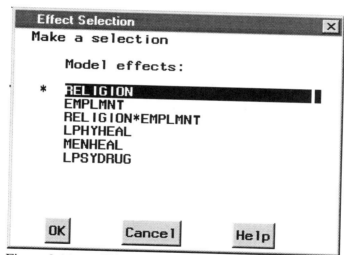

Figure 8.11   **Effect Selection** menu.

Clicking on RELIGION (to match decisions made in Section 8.6.2.1 of *UMS*) returns the **Output Statistics** menu of Figure 8.10, where clicking on **Least-square means...** produces a menu like that of Figure 8.10 for again selecting RELIGION.

Clicking on **Goback** twice after returning to the **Output Statistics** menu returns the **Analysis of Variance** dialog box, where clicking on the runner icon produces output identical to that of Tables 8.19 and 8.21 of *UMS*.

8.2.2 Homogeneity of Regression

This is demonstrated before assessing covariates because fewer menu modifications are required for this run in SAS/ASSIST. Choosing **Interactions...** from the **Model Effects** menu of Figure 8.6 allows the selection of interactions between effects and covariates as illustrated in Figure 8.12.

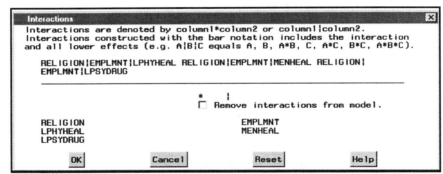

Figure 8.12   **Interactions** dialog box for evaluating homogeneity of regression.

These complex interactions are formed by clicking on a covariate, then |, then RELIGION|EMPLOYMENT. After clicking on **OK** and then **Goback** until the main **Analysis of Variance** dialog box appears, clicking on the runner icon produces the output of Table 8.25 in *UMS*.

8.2.3 Evaluation of Covariates

As is done for the syntax example in Section 8.6.2.2 of *UMS*, this analysis is done as a MANOVA, with the DV and CVs all treated as multiple DVs. This way, relationships among all four variables are shown. Thus the **Select Table Variables** of Figure 8.7 needs to be revisited to delete the three covariates. (You may also want to revisit the **Output Statistics** window to delete the requests for means and least square means.) At the main **Analysis of Variance** window (Figure 8.3), **Dependent:** variables are now selected to be ATTDRUG, LPHYHEAL, MENHEAL, and LPSYDRUG.

A return to the **Additional Options** menu (Figure 8.5) permits you to choose **Analysis type...**, which produces the **Analysis Type** menu of Figure 8.13.

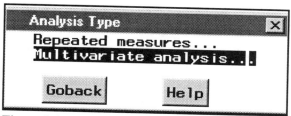

Figure 8.13   **Analysis Type** menu.

Choosing **Multivariate analysis...** produces the **Multivariate Analysis** menu of Figure 8.14, where **Hypothesis matrix...** is selected.

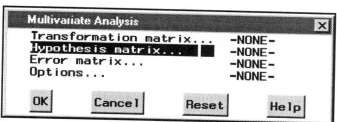

Figure 8.14   **Multivariate Analysis** menu to choose
Hypothesis matrix...

This produces the **Matrix Specification** menu of Figure 8.15, where **_ALL_** (test all main effects and the interaction) is selected.

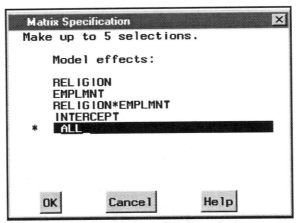

Figure 8.15   **Matrix Specification** menu.

Clicking on **OK** returns the **Multivariate Analysis** menu of Figure 8.14, where **Options...** is selected. This produces the **MANOVA Options** box of Figure 8.16, where **Print E matrix...** and **Print only multivariate tests...** are chosen.

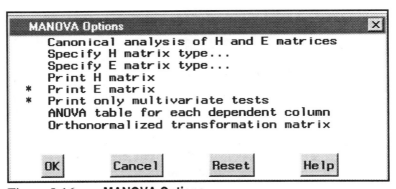

Figure 8.16   **MANOVA Options** menu.

After working back to the **Analysis of Variance** dialog box, clicking on the runner icon produces the output of Table 8.23 in *UMS*.

Chapter 9. Multivariate Analysis of Variance and Covariance

This chapter demonstrates multivariate analysis of variance and multivariate analysis of covariance using SAS for Windows, for the complete example of Chapter 9, *Using Multivariate Statistics*. The file to use is MANOVA.SAS7BDAT.

The examples evaluate several variables as a function of sex role identification: high vs. low femininity (FEM) and high vs. low masculinity (MASC). Dependent variables for the multivariate analysis of variance are self esteem (ESTEEM), locus of control (CONTROL), attitudes toward women's role (ATTROLE), socioeconomic level (SEL2), introversion-extraversion (INTEXT), and neuroticism (NEUROTIC).

Three of these variables, SEL2, CONTROL, and ATTROLE, serve as covariates in the multivariate analysis of covariance in which the other three variables remain DVs.

9.1   EVALUATION OF ASSUMPTIONS

Section 4.2 of this workbook shows how to find frequency distributions and histograms separately for each group. This data set is most easily split into groups by using the ANDRM variable, with its four levels corresponding to the two levels each of FEM and MASC. Frequencies and histograms are formed for each group as per Section 4.2. Figure 9.1 shows the **Distribution(Y)** dialog box for the six **Y** variables (only three of which appear in the display) by groups formed by ANDRM.

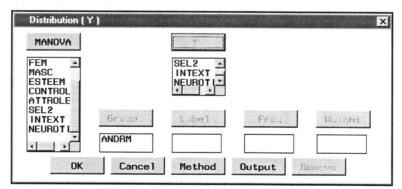

Figure 9.1   **Distribution(Y)** dialog box for MANOVA descriptive statistics.

Figure 9.2 shows the resulting descriptive and histograms for CONTROL for the ANDRM=1 group, which corresponds to low femininity and low masculinity (undifferentiated).

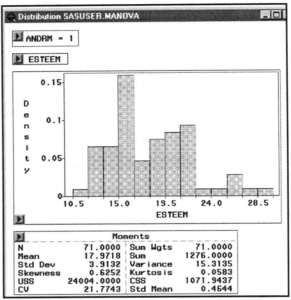

Figure 9.2   Descriptive statistics and histogram for CONTROL in undifferentiated group.

Section 4.2.2 shows how to evaluate linearity among DVs and covariates. Section 4.2.3 shows how to find within-groups multivariate outliers using separate regressions for each group and how to evaluate multicollinearity. SAS has no test for homogeneity of variance-covariance matrices. Instead, the guidelines of Section 9.3.2.4 of *UMS* are followed, examining the variances, covariances and cell sizes of the four groups. A pattern of large variances associated with large sample sizes is not particularly evident in this data set. Typically, it would be prudent to evaluate the results in terms of Pillai's criterion rather than Wilks' Lambda in the absence of further information about homogeneity of variance-covariance matrices. However, there is no difference between the two multivariate statistical criteria in this 2 x 2 design. Section 11.1 of this workbook shows how to conduct a formal test of homogeneity of variance-covariance matrices through PROC DISCRIM using batch processing.

Homogeneity of regression is not tested automatically in SAS programs but, as shown in Section 8.2.2, it can be evaluated by forming interactions between effects (main effects and interactions) and covariates through the analysis of covariance procedure. However, each covariate must be evaluated separately since covariates cannot be pooled. Further, separate runs are necessary for each DV in the stepdown analysis. The procedure first is demonstrated for the last stepdown test for MANOVA.

From the **SAS/ASSIST WorkPlace:** choose

> **Data Analysis**
>> **Anova**
>>> **Analysis of Variance...**

The DV, CONTROL, is selected by clicking on the **Dependent:** button in the **SAS/ASSIST:Analysis of Variance** dialog box and choosing CONTROL from the **Select Table Variables** box as per Figures 8.3 and 8.4. The IVs chosen after clicking on the **Classification:** button are FEM and MASC.

Covariates are chosen as per Figures 8.5 through 8.7. Here, Figure 9.3 shows the selection of ESTEEM, ATTROLE, NEUROTIC, and INTEXT as covariates.

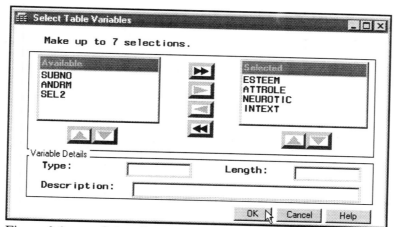

Figure 9.3   **Select Table Variables** list box for choosing covariates in MANOVA stepdown analysis.

Clicking on **OK** returns the **Model Effects** menu of Figure 8.7, where choosing **Interactions...** allows the selection of interactions between effects and covariates as illustrated in Figure 9.4.

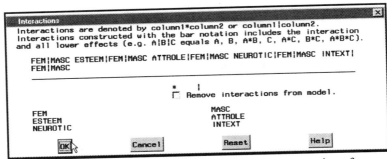

Figure 9.4 **Interactions** dialog box for homogeneity of regression for MANOVA stepdown analysis.

The FEM by MASC interaction is formed by clicking on FEM, then |, then MASC. Then each covariate interaction, in turn, is formed by clicking on the covariate, then |, then FEM|MASC. Clicking on **OK**, then **Goback** twice returns the **Analysis of Variance** dialog box, where clicking the runner icon produces *Output 9.1*.

Output 9.1 TESTS FOR HOMOGENEITY OF REGRESSION FOR MANOVA STEPDOWN ANALYSIS (PARTIAL OUTPUT SHOWING NEXT TO LAST TEST).

Source	DF	Type III SS	Mean Square	F Value	Pr > F
ESTEEM	1	14.51925903	14.51925903	11.42	0.0008
ATTROLE	1	0.66542399	0.66542399	0.52	0.4700
NEUROTIC	1	42.15665477	42.15665477	33.15	<.0001
INTEXT	1	2.18996351	2.18996351	1.72	0.1903
FEM	1	2.80168869	2.80168869	2.20	0.1387
MASC	1	3.02292033	3.02292033	2.38	0.1241
FEM*MASC	1	0.00004978	0.00004978	0.00	0.9950
ESTEEM*FEM	1	0.13300417	0.13300417	0.10	0.7466
ESTEEM*MASC	1	2.17334725	2.17334725	1.71	0.1920
ESTEEM*FEM*MASC	1	0.72492652	0.72492652	0.57	0.4508
ATTROLE*FEM	1	1.50901141	1.50901141	1.19	0.2768
ATTROLE*MASC	1	0.01751470	0.01751470	0.01	0.9067
ATTROLE*FEM*MASC	1	0.05635275	0.05635275	0.04	0.8334
NEUROTIC*FEM	1	0.60013689	0.60013689	0.47	0.4926
NEUROTIC*MASC	1	0.60177935	0.60177935	0.47	0.4920
NEUROTIC*FEM*MASC	1	0.66835390	0.66835390	0.53	0.4690
INTEXT*FEM	1	0.84111896	0.84111896	0.66	0.4166
INTEXT*MASC	1	2.61147781	2.61147781	2.05	0.1528
INTEXT*FEM*MASC	1	3.84422618	3.84422618	3.02	0.0830

The output shows no threat of violation of homogeneity of regression.

Figure 9.5 shows the **Analysis of Variance** dialog box with three DVs selected (ESTEEM, INTEXT, and NEUROTIC) for the overall test of homogeneity of regression for MANCOVA.

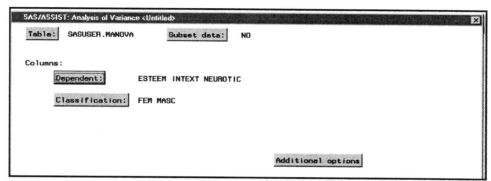

Figure 9.5   **Analysis of Variance** dialog box for MANCOVA.

Choosing **Additional options** and then **Model effects...** allows selection of **Covariates...** as per Figure 8.7. The **Select Table Variables** list box showing selection of CONTROL, ATTROLE, and SEL2 as covariates appears in Figure 9.6.

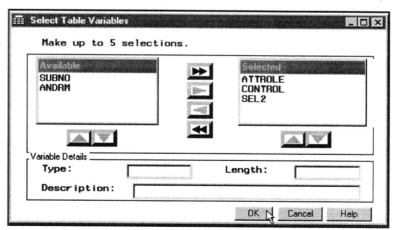

Figure 9.6   **Select Table Variables** list box for selecting covariates for MANCOVA.

Clicking on **OK** returns the **Model Effects** menu, in which clicking on **Interactions...** allows formation of the appropriate interactions, as seen in Figure 9.7. (Note that you need to first click on **Remove Interactions from model** if you are continuing from an earlier run with different interactions.)

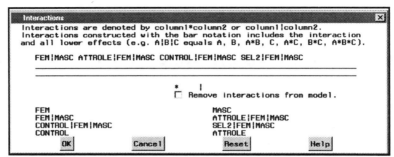

Figure 9.7   **Interactions** dialog box for testing homogeneity of regression for overall MANCOVA.

Clicking on **OK** and then **Goback** twice returns the **Analysis of Variance** dialog box where clicking the runner icon produces *Output 9.2*.

Output 9.2 TESTS FOR HOMOGENEITY OF REGRESSION FOR MANCOVA ANALYSIS (PARTIAL OUTPUT SHOWING OVERALL TEST FOR ESTEEM).

Source	DF	Type III SS	Mean Square	F Value	Pr > F
ATTROLE	1	83.8848081	83.8848081	7.78	0.0056
CONTROL	1	442.5058258	442.5058258	41.06	<.0001
SEL2	1	0.4312639	0.4312639	0.04	0.8416
FEM	1	22.0976914	22.0976914	2.05	0.1531
MASC	1	9.9028232	9.9028232	0.92	0.3384
FEM*MASC	1	7.4510689	7.4510689	0.69	0.4063
ATTROLE*FEM	1	3.7220831	3.7220831	0.35	0.5571
ATTROLE*MASC	1	1.4710977	1.4710977	0.14	0.7120
ATTROLE*FEM*MASC	1	1.7896268	1.7896268	0.17	0.6839
CONTROL*FEM	1	30.0006357	30.0006357	2.78	0.0961
CONTROL*MASC	1	3.3828389	3.3828389	0.31	0.5757
CONTROL*FEM*MASC	1	0.2193496	0.2193496	0.02	0.8866
SEL2*FEM	1	6.1289610	6.1289610	0.57	0.4513
SEL2*MASC	1	14.1077111	14.1077111	1.31	0.2534
SEL2*FEM*MASC	1	42.0812101	42.0812101	3.90	0.0489

The three-way interactions are the tests of homogeneity of regression. The Pr > F value of 0.0489 for the SEL2 by FEM by MASC interaction is within tolerable limits considering the multitude of tests in this analysis. An appropriate critical α level might be about .006. The remaining DVs show no cause for concern.

9.2 MULTIVARIATE ANALYSIS OF VARIANCE

From the **SAS/ASSIST WorkPlace:**

> **Data Analysis**
>> **Anova**
>>> **Analysis of Variance...**

produces the **SAS/ASSIST: Analysis of Variance** dialog box of Figure 8.3.

The **Dependent:** selections are ESTEEM, ATTROLE, NEUROTIC, INTEXT, CONTROL, and SEL2, as seen in Figure 9.8.

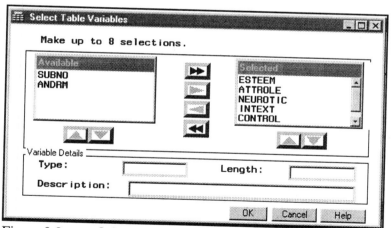

Figure 9.8   **Select Table Variables** list box for selecting DVs in MANOVA.

Clicking on **OK** returns the **Analysis of Variance** dialog box, where clicking on **Classification:** allows choice of FEM and MASC as IVs. The order of listing (first FEM, then MASC) is important for this sequential (Method 3) approach to dealing with unequal-*n*. Clicking on **OK** returns the **Analysis of Variance** dialog box of Figure 9.9.

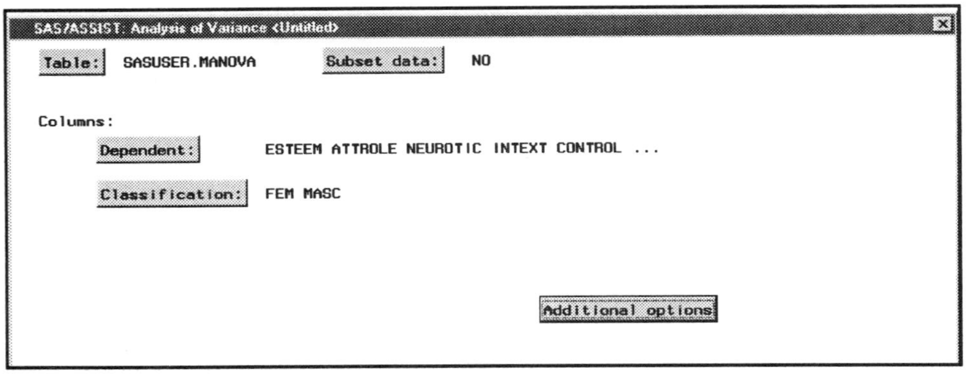

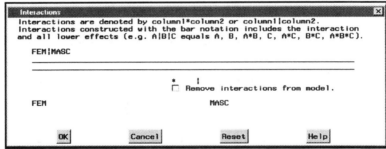

Figure 9.9   **Analysis of Variance** dialog box for MANOVA.

Clicking on the **Additional options** button produces the **Additional Options** menu of Figure 8.5, where clicking on **Model effects...** produces the **Model Effects** menu of Figure 8.6. Clicking on **Interactions...** allows the formation of the FEM by MASC interaction, as seen in Figure 9.10.

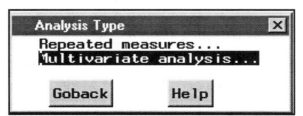

Figure 9.10   **Interactions** dialog box for FEM by MASC interaction for MANOVA.

Clicking on FEM, then |, then MASC requests tests for the two main effects as well as the interaction.

Clicking on **OK** and then **Goback** returns the **Additional Options** menu, where clicking on **Analysis type...** produces the **Analysis Type** menu, as seen in Figure 9.11.

Figure 9.11   **Analysis Type** menu for MANOVA.

Clicking on **Multivariate analysis...** produces the **Multivariate Analysis** menu of Figure 9.12.

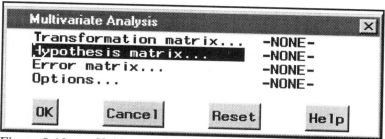

Figure 9.12   **Multivariate Analysis** menu for MANOVA.

Clicking on **Hypothesis matrix...** brings up the **Matrix Specification** menu of Figure 9.13, in which **_ALL_** is selected.

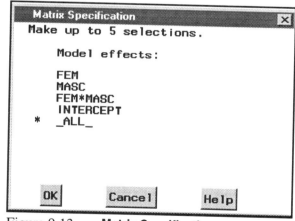

Figure 9.13   **Matrix Specification** menu for MANOVA.

Clicking on **OK** returns the **Multivariate Analysis** menu, where clicking on **OK** and then **Goback** returns the **Additional Options** menu of Figure 8.6. Clicking on **Model options...** produces the **Model Options** dialog box of Figure 9.14, where a choice is made to ☑**Print Type I Sums of Squares.**

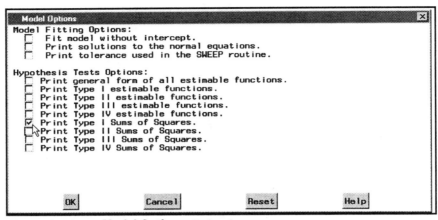

Figure 9.14   **Model Options** dialog box.

Clicking on **OK** returns the **Additional Options** dialog box, where clicking on **Output statistics...** produces the **Output Statistics** list, where clicking on **Means...** produces the **Effect Selection** dialog box (as per Figure 8.11). The FEM*MASC effect is selected.

Clicking on **OK** and then **Goback** returns the **Analysis of Variance** dialog box, where clicking the runner icon produces *Output 9.3*.

Output 9.3 MULTIVARIATE ANALYSIS OF VARIANCE OF ESTEEM, CONTROL, ATTROLE, SEL2, INTEXT, AND NEUROTIC AS A FUNCTION OF FEMININITY, MASCULINITY, AND THEIR INTERACTION (SELECTED OUTPUT).

The GLM Procedure

Class Level Information

Class	Levels	Values
FEM	2	1 2
MASC	2	1 2

Number of observations   369

NOTE: Observations with missing values will not be included in this analysis. Thus, only 368
      observations can be used in this analysis.

Dependent Variable: ESTEEM   Self-esteem

Source	DF	Sum of Squares	Mean Square	F Value	Pr > F
Model	3	1098.553065	366.184355	29.33	<.0001
Error	364	4544.446935	12.484744		
Corrected Total	367	5643.000000			

R-Square	Coeff Var	Root MSE	ESTEEM Mean
0.194675	22.43413	3.533376	15.75000

Source	DF	Type I SS	Mean Square	F Value	Pr > F
FEM	1	101.4653561	101.4653561	8.13	0.0046
MASC	1	979.6008626	979.6008626	78.46	<.0001
FEM*MASC	1	17.4868457	17.4868457	1.40	0.2374

Dependent Variable: ATTROLE   Attitudes toward role of women

Source	DF	Sum of Squares	Mean Square	F Value	Pr > F
Model	3	2074.44130	691.48043	17.83	<.0001
Error	364	14115.12120	38.77781		
Corrected Total	367	16189.56250			

R-Square	Coeff Var	Root MSE	ATTROLE Mean
0.128134	17.82378	6.227183	34.93750

Source	DF	Type I SS	Mean Square	F Value	Pr > F
FEM	1	610.888600	610.888600	15.75	<.0001
MASC	1	1426.756753	1426.756753	36.79	<.0001
FEM*MASC	1	36.795942	36.795942	0.95	0.3306

Dependent Variable: NEUROTIC   Neuroticism

Source	DF	Sum of Squares	Mean Square	F Value	Pr > F
Model	3	223.790769	74.596923	3.03	0.0296

Source	DF	Sum of Squares	Mean Square		
Error	364	8973.676622	24.652958		
Corrected Total	367	9197.467391			

R-Square	Coeff Var	Root MSE	NEUROTIC Mean
0.024332	56.99265	4.965174	8.711957

Source	DF	Type I SS	Mean Square	F Value	Pr > F
FEM	1	44.0544218	44.0544218	1.79	0.1821
MASC	1	179.5339579	179.5339579	7.28	0.0073
FEM*MASC	1	0.2023892	0.2023892	0.01	0.9279

Dependent Variable: INTEXT   Introversion-extraversion

Source	DF	Sum of Squares	Mean Square	F Value	Pr > F
Model	3	415.190566	138.396855	10.75	<.0001
Error	364	4684.178999	12.868624		
Corrected Total	367	5099.369565			

R-Square	Coeff Var	Root MSE	INTEXT Mean
0.081420	30.72908	3.587286	11.67391

Source	DF	Type I SS	Mean Square	F Value	Pr > F
FEM	1	87.7599580	87.7599580	6.82	0.0094
MASC	1	327.4079726	327.4079726	25.44	<.0001
FEM*MASC	1	0.0226356	0.0226356	0.00	0.9666

Dependent Variable: CONTROL   Locus-of-control

Source	DF	Sum of Squares	Mean Square	F Value	Pr > F
Model	3	15.5856851	5.1952284	3.24	0.0223
Error	364	584.1425757	1.6047873		
Corrected Total	367	599.7282609			

	R-Square	Coeff Var	Root MSE	CONTROL Mean
	0.025988	18.84330	1.266802	6.722826

Source	DF	Type I SS	Mean Square	F Value	Pr > F
FEM	1	2.83106461	2.83106461	1.76	0.1849
MASC	1	11.85923432	11.85923432	7.39	0.0069
FEM*MASC	1	0.89538621	0.89538621	0.56	0.4556

Dependent Variable: SEL2   Socioeconomic level

Source	DF	Sum of Squares	Mean Square	F Value	Pr > F
Model	3	1467.9703	489.3234	0.75	0.5215
Error	364	236708.9663	650.2994		
Corrected Total	367	238176.9366			

	R-Square	Coeff Var	Root MSE	SEL2 Mean
	0.006163	62.23637	25.50097	40.97438

Source	DF	Type I SS	Mean Square	F Value	Pr > F
FEM	1	9.006913	9.006913	0.01	0.9064
MASC	1	1105.381962	1105.381962	1.70	0.1931
FEM*MASC	1	353.581434	353.581434	0.54	0.4614

MANOVA Test Criteria and Exact F Statistics for the Hypothesis of No Overall FEM Effect
H = Type I SSCP Matrix for FEM
E = Error SSCP Matrix

S=1   M=2   N=178.5

Statistic	Value	F Value	Num DF	Den DF	Pr > F
Wilks' Lambda	0.91899207	5.27	6	359	<.0001
Pillai's Trace	0.08100793	5.27	6	359	<.0001
Hotelling-Lawley Trace	0.08814867	5.27	6	359	<.0001
Roy's Greatest Root	0.08814867	5.27	6	359	<.0001

MANOVA Test Criteria and Exact F Statistics for the Hypothesis of No Overall MASC Effect
H = Type I SSCP Matrix for MASC
E = Error SSCP Matrix

S=1   M=2   N=178.5

Statistic	Value	F Value	Num DF	Den DF	Pr > F
Wilks' Lambda	0.75636584	19.27	6	359	<.0001
Pillai's Trace	0.24363416	19.27	6	359	<.0001
Hotelling-Lawley Trace	0.32211152	19.27	6	359	<.0001
Roy's Greatest Root	0.32211152	19.27	6	359	<.0001

MANOVA Test Criteria and Exact F Statistics for the Hypothesis of No Overall FEM*MASC Effect
H = Type I SSCP Matrix for FEM*MASC
E = Error SSCP Matrix

S=1   M=2   N=178.5

Statistic	Value	F Value	Num DF	Den DF	Pr > F
Wilks' Lambda	0.99183935	0.49	6	359	0.8141
Pillai's Trace	0.00816065	0.49	6	359	0.8141
Hotelling-Lawley Trace	0.00822779	0.49	6	359	0.8141
Roy's Greatest Root	0.00822779	0.49	6	359	0.8141

10:55 Sunday, August 1, 1999   11

The GLM Procedure

Level of FEM	Level of MASC	N	ESTEEM Mean	ESTEEM Std Dev	ATTROLE Mean	ATTROLE Std Dev
1	1	71	17.9718310	3.91324429	34.6760563	5.96603397
1	2	36	13.8055556	3.94113431	29.4722222	5.57282237
2	1	172	16.4883721	3.49684632	37.0348837	6.29572894
2	2	89	13.3370787	3.08568476	33.3033708	6.53557484

Level of FEM	Level of MASC	N	NEUROTIC Mean	NEUROTIC Std Dev	INTEXT Mean	INTEXT Std Dev
1	1	71	9.77464789	5.14419835	10.2323944	3.69636017
1	2	36	8.22222222	4.89379263	12.2500000	3.59861084
2	1	172	8.98255814	5.11673534	11.3110465	3.66715229
2	2	89	7.53932584	4.53034260	13.2921348	3.32843209

Level of FEM	Level of MASC	N	CONTROL Mean	CONTROL Std Dev	SEL2 Mean	SEL2 Std Dev
1	1	71	7.04225352	1.34628186	38.4076461	25.2873969
1	2	36	6.50000000	1.18321596	45.3103178	28.0048722
2	1	172	6.77325581	1.26619792	40.2770766	24.6760482
2	2	89	6.46067416	1.23450560	42.6157306	26.1930308

Two univariate ANOVA tables appear for each DV, first with all effects combined, and then with the two main effects and interaction reported. Then the multivariate tables appear for FEM, MASC, and the interaction. Finally, unadjusted cell means and standard deviations are reported for each cell.

Pooled within-cell correlations among DVs are available through PROC DISCRIM using batch processing, as shown in Section 11.2.1 of this workbook.

Stepdown analysis is not directly available in SAS. Instead, individual analyses of covariance are performed for each DV (except the one with highest priority), with higher priority DVs treated as covariates. Thus, the ANCOVA for ATTROLE uses ESTEEM as a covariate, the ANCOVA for NEUROTIC uses ATTROLE and ESTEEM as covariates, and so on.

The process for INTEXT is demonstrated here. First, clear out all choices made for the omnibus MANOVA. Then, select INTEXT as the **Dependent:** variable and FEM and MASC as the **Classification:** variables. Clicking on the **Additional options** button, then **Model effects...** and then **Covariates...** produces the **Select Table Variables** list box to choose ESTEEM, ATTROLE, and NEUROTIC, as seen in Figure 9.15.

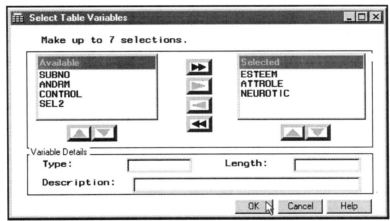

Figure 9.15   **Select Table Variables** list box to choose covariates for stepdown analysis of INTEXT.

Clicking on **OK** returns the **Model Effects** menu, where clicking on **Interactions...** produces the **Interaction** dialog box, where the FEM|MASC interaction is specified as per Figure 9.10.

Least square means may be requested at this point, so that adjusted means are available if any effects turn out to be statistically significant. This is done by choosing **Output statistics...** from the **Additional Options** menu of Figure 8.10. Clicking on **Least-squares means...** produces the **Effect Selection** menu where, with great foresight, the effect chosen is MASC. (Note that there is a significant stepdown effect for MASC on INTEXT in Table 9.18 of *UMS*. In the absence of such precognition, separate runs would be necessary for adjusted means for each effect.)

One additional complication arises because CONTROL, with its missing value, is not considered in this analysis. Clicking on **OK** and **Goback** twice returns the **Analysis of Variance** dialog box, where the **Subset data:** button is clicked, producing the **Subset Data** dialog box of Figure 4.24. Clicking on **WHERE clause:** produces a dialog box that permits inclusion of the cases with CONTROL ^= ., as per Figure 9.16.

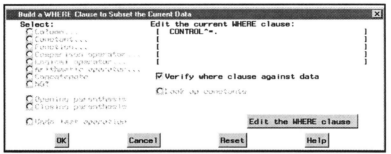

Figure 9.16   **Build a WHERE clause to Subset the Current Data** dialog box to delete case with missing CONTROL value.

Clicking on **OK** and **Goback** returns the **Analysis of Variance** dialog box, where clicking on the runner icon produces *Output 9.4*.

Output 9.4 STEPDOWN ANALYSIS FOR INTEXT WITH ADJUSTED MEANS FOR THE MAIN EFFECT OF MASCULINITY (SELECTED OUTPUT).

```
                       The GLM Procedure

                   Class Level Information

           Class          Levels      Values

           FEM                 2      1 2

           MASC                2      1 2


           Number of observations      368


                   The GLM Procedure
```

Dependent Variable: INTEXT   Introversion-extraversion

Source	DF	Sum of Squares	Mean Square	F Value	Pr > F
Model	6	560.943728	93.490621	7.44	<.0001
Error	361	4538.425837	12.571817		
Corrected Total	367	5099.369565			

R-Square	Coeff Var	Root MSE	INTEXT Mean
0.110003	30.37264	3.545676	11.67391

Source	DF	Type I SS	Mean Square	F Value	Pr > F
ESTEEM	1	357.3276626	357.3276626	28.42	<.0001
ATTROLE	1	1.9118719	1.9118719	0.15	0.6968
NEUROTIC	1	14.2842176	14.2842176	1.14	0.2872
FEM	1	46.5733690	46.5733690	3.70	0.0550
MASC	1	140.5855093	140.5855093	11.18	0.0009
FEM*MASC	1	0.2610981	0.2610981	0.02	0.8855

The GLM Procedure
Least Squares Means

MASC	INTEXT LSMEAN
1	11.0108740
2	12.4582424

Note that results differ slightly from those of Tables 9.18 and 9.20 due to differences in algorithms for the programs.

Similar procedures are used for other adjusted means, including means for the highest priority effect. That is, means must be adjusted for order of effects (FEM, then MASC, then interaction) as well as any covariates. The only unadjusted means would be those for the highest level effect (FEM) and the highest priority DV (ESTEEM). Each set of marginal or cell means require a separate run.

9.3   MULTIVARIATE ANALYSIS OF COVARIANCE

From the **SAS/ASSIST WorkPlace:** select

> **> Data Analysis**
>   **> Anova**
>   **> Analysis of Variance...**

producing the **SAS/ASSIST: Analysis of Variance** dialog box of Figure 8.4.

The **Dependent:** selections are ESTEEM, INTEXT, and NEUROTIC. The **Classification:** choices are FEM (first) and then MASC. Order is important in this sequential approach to dealing with unequal-*n*. Choices are shown in the **Analysis of Variance** dialog box in Figure 9.17.

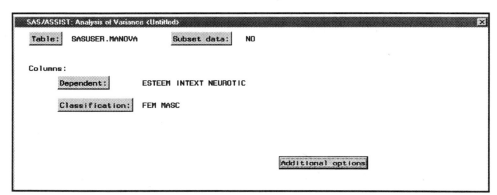

Figure 9.17   **SAS/ASSIST: Analysis of Variance** dialog box for MANCOVA.

Clicking on **Additional options** produces the **Additional Options** menu of Figure 8.6, where clicking on **Model effects...** produces the **Model Effects** menu of Figure 8.7. Clicking on **Covariates...** brings up the **Select Table Variables** list box, in which CONTROL, ATTROLE, and SEL2 are selected, as shown in Figure 9.18.

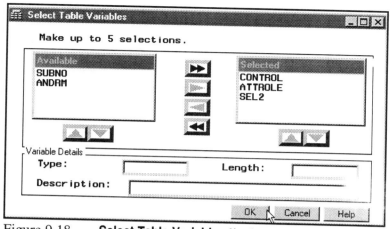

Figure 9.18   **Select Table Variables** list box for selecting
covariates in MANCOVA.

Clicking on **OK** returns the **Model Effects** menu, where clicking on **Interactions**... allows the formation of
the FEM by MASC interaction, as per Figure 9.19.

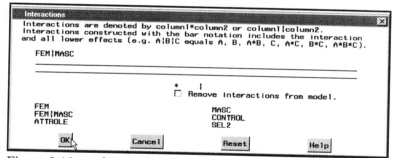

Figure 9.19   **Interactions** dialog box for forming FEM by
MASC interaction for MANCOVA.

First click on FEM, then |, then MASC to form the interaction of interest. Clicking on **OK** and then
Goback returns the **Additional Options** menu, where clicking on **Analysis type...** produces the **Analysis
Type** menu of Figure 9.11.

Procedures illustrated in Figures 9.11 through 9.14 allow specification of multivariate analysis in
which _ALL_ effects are included, and Type I Sums of Squares are printed. After returning to the
Analysis of Variance dialog box, clicking the runner icon produces *Output 9.5.*

MULTIVARIATE ANALYSIS OF COVARIANCE OF ESTEEM, INTEXT, AND NEUROTIC AS A FUNCTION OF FEMININITY, MASCULINITY, AND THEIR INTERACTION; COVARIATES ARE ATTROLE, CONTROL, AND SEL2 (SELECTED OUTPUT).

```
                        The GLM Procedure

                     Class Level Information

            Class       Levels    Values

            FEM              2     1 2

            MASC             2     1 2


                  Number of observations    369
```

NOTE: Observations with missing values will not be included in this analysis. Thus, only 368 observations can be used in this analysis.

```
                        The GLM Procedure
```

Dependent Variable: ESTEEM   Self-esteem

```
                                   Sum of
      Source              DF       Squares     Mean Square    F Value    Pr > F

      Model                6   1759.395104      293.232517      27.26    <.0001

      Error              361   3883.604896       10.757908

      Corrected Total    367   5643.000000
```

```
         R-Square    Coeff Var    Root MSE    ESTEEM Mean

         0.311784    20.82492     3.279925    15.75000
```

Source	DF	Type I SS	Mean Square	F Value	Pr > F
CONTROL	1	806.5657091	806.5657091	74.97	<.0001
ATTROLE	1	276.1911562	276.1911562	25.67	<.0001
SEL2	1	3.8196345	3.8196345	0.36	0.5516
FEM	1	134.5656365	134.5656365	12.51	0.0005
MASC	1	531.0336538	531.0336538	49.36	<.0001
FEM*MASC	1	7.2193138	7.2193138	0.67	0.4132

Dependent Variable: INTEXT   Introversion-extraversion

Source	DF	Sum of Squares	Mean Square	F Value	Pr > F
Model	6	458.856614	76.476102	5.95	<.0001
Error	361	4640.512951	12.854607		
Corrected Total	367	5099.369565			

R-Square	Coeff Var	Root MSE	INTEXT Mean
0.089983	30.71234	3.585332	11.67391

Source	DF	Type I SS	Mean Square	F Value	Pr > F
CONTROL	1	77.6230768	77.6230768	6.04	0.0145
ATTROLE	1	8.0103785	8.0103785	0.62	0.4304
SEL2	1	17.9686319	17.9686319	1.40	0.2379
FEM	1	90.5203243	90.5203243	7.04	0.0083
MASC	1	264.7082994	264.7082994	20.59	<.0001
FEM*MASC	1	0.0259032	0.0259032	0.00	0.9642

Dependent Variable: NEUROTIC   Neuroticism

Source	DF	Sum of Squares	Mean Square	F Value	Pr > F
Model	6	1607.951356	267.991893	12.75	<.0001
Error	361	7589.516036	21.023590		
Corrected Total	367	9197.467391			

R-Square	Coeff Var	Root MSE	NEUROTIC Mean
0.174825	52.63053	4.585149	8.711957

Source	DF	Type I SS	Mean Square	F Value	Pr > F
CONTROL	1	1487.850717	1487.850717	70.77	<.0001
ATTROLE	1	50.583225	50.583225	2.41	0.1217
SEL2	1	1.674284	1.674284	0.08	0.7779
FEM	1	30.125068	30.125068	1.43	0.2321
MASC	1	36.191700	36.191700	1.72	0.1903
FEM*MASC	1	1.526360	1.526360	0.07	0.7877

MANOVA Test Criteria and Exact F Statistics for the Hypothesis of No Overall CONTROL Effect

115

E = Error SSCP Matrix

S=1   M=0.5   N=178.5

Statistic	Value	F Value	Num DF	Den DF	Pr > F
Wilks' Lambda	0.75195535	39.47	3	359	<.0001
Pillai's Trace	0.24804465	39.47	3	359	<.0001
Hotelling-Lawley Trace	0.32986620	39.47	3	359	<.0001
Roy's Greatest Root	0.32986620	39.47	3	359	<.0001

MANOVA Test Criteria and Exact F Statistics for the Hypothesis of No Overall ATTROLE Effect
H = Type I SSCP Matrix for ATTROLE
E = Error SSCP Matrix

S=1   M=0.5   N=178.5

Statistic	Value	F Value	Num DF	Den DF	Pr > F
Wilks' Lambda	0.93339539	8.54	3	359	<.0001
Pillai's Trace	0.06660461	8.54	3	359	<.0001
Hotelling-Lawley Trace	0.07135734	8.54	3	359	<.0001
Roy's Greatest Root	0.07135734	8.54	3	359	<.0001

MANOVA Test Criteria and Exact F Statistics for the Hypothesis of No Overall SEL2 Effect
H = Type I SSCP Matrix for SEL2
E = Error SSCP Matrix

S=1   M=0.5   N=178.5

Statistic	Value	F Value	Num DF	Den DF	Pr > F
Wilks' Lambda	0.99525704	0.57	3	359	0.6349
Pillai's Trace	0.00474296	0.57	3	359	0.6349
Hotelling-Lawley Trace	0.00476556	0.57	3	359	0.6349
Roy's Greatest Root	0.00476556	0.57	3	359	0.6349

MANOVA Test Criteria and Exact F Statistics for the Hypothesis of No Overall FEM Effect
H = Type I SSCP Matrix for FEM
E = Error SSCP Matrix

S=1   M=0.5   N=178.5

Statistic	Value	F Value	Num DF	Den DF	Pr > F
Wilks' Lambda	0.95413551	5.75	3	359	0.0007
Pillai's Trace	0.04586449	5.75	3	359	0.0007
Hotelling-Lawley Trace	0.04806915	5.75	3	359	0.0007
Roy's Greatest Root	0.04806915	5.75	3	359	0.0007

MANOVA Test Criteria and Exact F Statistics for the Hypothesis of No Overall MASC Effect

116

H = Type I SSCP Matrix for MASC
E = Error SSCP Matrix

S=1   M=0.5   N=178.5

Statistic	Value	F Value	Num DF	Den DF	Pr > F
Wilks' Lambda	0.85359576	20.52	3	359	<.0001
Pillai's Trace	0.14640424	20.52	3	359	<.0001
Hotelling-Lawley Trace	0.17151472	20.52	3	359	<.0001
Roy's Greatest Root	0.17151472	20.52	3	359	<.0001

Characteristic Roots and Vectors of: E Inverse * H, where

MANOVA Test Criteria and Exact F Statistics for the Hypothesis of No Overall FEM*MASC Effect
H = Type I SSCP Matrix for FEM*MASC
E = Error SSCP Matrix

S=1   M=0.5   N=178.5

Statistic	Value	F Value	Num DF	Den DF	Pr > F
Wilks' Lambda	0.99737034	0.32	3	359	0.8142
Pillai's Trace	0.00262966	0.32	3	359	0.8142
Hotelling-Lawley Trace	0.00263659	0.32	3	359	0.8142
Roy's Greatest Root	0.00263659	0.32	3	359	0.8142

Two univariate tables appear for each DV, the first with all effects combined, and then the second with the individual effects reported: each covariate in turn, the main effects, and the interaction. Note that these results differ slightly from those of Table 9.26 of *UMS* due to differences in algorithms used for sequential sums of squares among programs.

Multivariate tests follow, with tests for the covariates appearing first. For example, the multivariate test for CONTROL tests the relationship between that covariate and the combined DVs. Note that CONTROL and ATTROLE show multivariate effects; SEL2 does not. It is therefore useful to look at the univariate tests for the three DVs to see which are related to CONTROL and ATTROLE. These test that CONTROL and ATTROLE are related to ESTEEM, and CONTROL is related to INTEXT and NEUROTIC. Multivariate tests of the two main effects and interaction show the same substantive results as in Table 9.24 of *UMS*, but with minor variations due to differences in algorithms.

Stepdown analysis is not directly available in SAS. Instead, individual analyses of covariance are performed on INTEXT and NEUROTIC, with higher priority DVs as well as covariates serving as "covariates". The procedure for INTEXT is demonstrated here.

First, select INTEXT as the **Dependent:** and FEM and MASC as the **Classification:** variables, keeping the selection of the FEM by MASC interaction (Figure 9.19). Clicking on the **Additional options** button, then **Model effects...** and then **Covariates...** produces the **Select Table Variables** list box to choose CONTROL, ATTROLE, SEL2 (the original covariates), and ESTEEM (the higher priority DV), as seen in Figure 9.20.

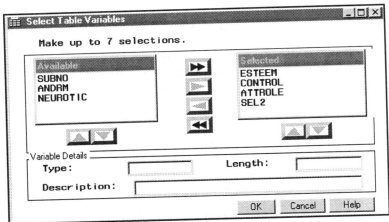

Figure 9.20   **Select Table Variables** list box for selecting covariates for stepdown analysis of INTEXT in MANCOVA.

Least squares means may be requested at this point, so that adjusted means are available if any effects turn out to be significant. However, only least squares means for one main effect or the interaction may be requested, with the others requiring separate runs. We will choose to request least squares means for the MASC effect, knowing beforehand that the stepdown effect of MASC is significant for INTEXT (from Table 9.27 in *UMS*). This is done by choosing **Output statistics...** from the **Additional Options** menu of Figure 8.10. Clicking on **Least-squares means...** produces the **Effect Selection** menu, where the effect chosen is MASC.

Working back to the **Analysis of Variance** dialog box and clicking on the runner icon produces *Output 9.6*.

The GLM Procedure

Class Level Information

Class	Levels	Values
FEM	2	1 2
MASC	2	1 2

Number of observations   369

NOTE: Observations with missing values will not be included in this analysis. Thus, only 368 observations can be used in this analysis.

Dependent Variable: INTEXT   Introversion-extraversion

Source	DF	Sum of Squares	Mean Square	F Value	Pr > F
Model	7	560.926740	80.132391	6.36	<.0001
Error	360	4538.442825	12.606786		
Corrected Total	367	5099.369565			

R-Square	Coeff Var	Root MSE	INTEXT Mean
0.109999	30.41485	3.550604	11.67391

Source	DF	Type I SS	Mean Square	F Value	Pr > F
CONTROL	1	77.6230768	77.6230768	6.16	0.0135
ATTROLE	1	8.0103785	8.0103785	0.64	0.4259
SEL2	1	17.9686319	17.9686319	1.43	0.2333
ESTEEM	1	272.5884163	272.5884163	21.62	<.0001
FEM	1	45.9375991	45.9375991	3.64	0.0571
MASC	1	138.4434421	138.4434421	10.98	0.0010
FEM*MASC	1	0.3551957	0.3551957	0.03	0.8668

Least Squares Means

MASC	INTEXT LSMEAN
1	11.0169871
2	12.4496506

119

Similar procedures are used for other adjusted means. For example, marginal means on ESTEEM for the two levels of FEM would be adjusted only for the three original covariates.

Chapter 10. Profile Analysis of Repeated Measures

This chapter demonstrates profile analyses of repeated measures using SAS for Windows, for the complete examples of Chapter 10, *Using Multivariate Statistics*. The files to use are PROFILE.SAS7BDAT and DBLMULT.SAS7BDAT.

10.1   PROFILE ANALYSIS OF SUBSCALES OF THE WISC

This example assesses variability in subtest scores on the Wechsler Intelligence Scale for Children (WISC) as a function of preference of learning-disabled children for age of playmates (AGEMATE). Levels of AGEMATE are whether children are reported to prefer (1) playmates younger than themselves, (2) playmates older than themselves, or (3) playmates about the same age or no preference. WISC subtests used are information (INFO), comprehension (COMP), arithmetic (ARITH), similarities (SIMIL), vocabulary (VOCAB), digit span (DIGIT), picture completion (PICTCOMP), picture arrangement (PARANG), block design (BLOCK), object assembly (OBJECT), and CODING.

SAS/ASSIST is unable to process more than eight DVs (eight levels of the repeated-measures variable). The complete example of Chapter 10 of *Using Multivariate Statistics* has 11 levels. Therefore, the example is done through SAS batch processing, just as in Section 10.6.1.2 of *UMS* . Section 10.1.2. of this workbook contains an example of profile analysis with only the first six WISC subtests (INFO through DIGIT) to demonstrate the procedure using SAS ASSIST.

10.1.1   Evaluation of Assumptions

Section 4.2 of this workbook shows how to find frequency distributions and histograms separately for each AGEMATE group. Note that a group is formed for those cases with missing values on the grouping variable (AGEMATE).   Missing values for *Y* variables are not explicitly shown in these distributions, but may be found by subtracting displayed **N** for each variable from the known sample size for each group.

If unknown, sample size for each group may be found through the **Interactive Data Analysis** procedure by choosing the grouping variable as the **Y** variable in the **Distribution(Y)** dialog box, and requesting a table of ☑**Frequency Counts** in the **Output** dialog box, as seen in Figure 10.1.

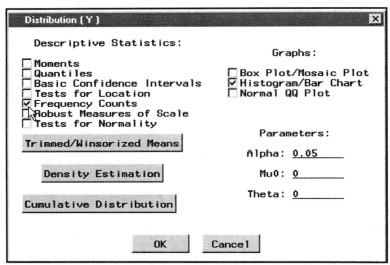

Figure 10.1   **Distribution(Y)** dialog box for determining group
sample sizes.

This procedure produces the histogram and frequency table of Figure 10.2, showing sample sizes for the three AGEMATE groups.

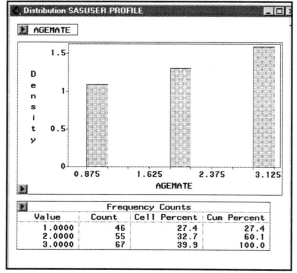

Figure 10.2   Sample sizes for three
AGEMATE groups.

Section 4.2.2 shows how to evaluate linearity among variables. Section 4.2.3 shows how to find within-groups multivariate outliers using separate regressions for each group and how to evaluate multicollinearity. SAS/ASSIST has no test for homogeneity of variance-covariance matrices. However, sample sizes in this analysis are not particularly discrepant, nor are substantial differences noted among variances. Therefore there is no concern with heterogeneity of variance-covariance matrices. Section 11.1 of this workbook shows how to conduct a formal test of homogeneity of variance-covariance matrices through PROC DISCRIM using batch processing.

10.1.2 Profile Analysis of Six Subtests

From the **SAS/ASSIST WorkPlace:** select

> **> Data Analysis**
>   **> Anova**
>   **> Analysis of Variance...**

This produces the **SAS/ASSIST: Analysis of Variance** dialog box of Figure 8.3. The **Dependent:** variable selections are INFO to DIGIT, and the **Classification:** variable is AGEMATE, as seen in Figure 10.3.

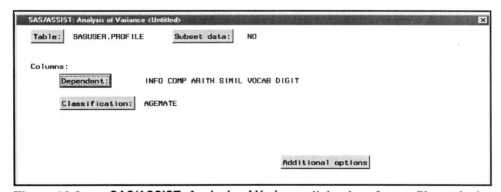

Figure 10.3   **SAS/ASSIST: Analysis of Variance** dialog box for profile analysis.

Clicking on the **Additional options** button produces the **Additional Options** menu of Figure 8.6, where clicking on **Analysis type...** produces the **Analysis Type** menu of Figure 9.11. Clicking on **Repeated measures...** brings up the **Repeated Measures** menu of Figure 10.4.

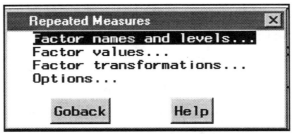

Figure 10.4   **Repeated Measures** menu.

Clicking on **Factor names and levels...** produces the **Repeated Measures Factors** dialog box of Figure 10.5, where SUBTEST is entered as the **Factor Name** and 6 is entered as the **Number of Levels.**

```
Repeated Measures Factors                    [X]
    Factor         Factor        Number of
    Number         Name          Levels

      1            SUBTEST       6
      2            _____     _____
      3            _____     _____
      4            _____     _____
      5            _____     _____

   OK      Cancel      Reset       Help
```

Figure 10.5   **Repeated Measures Factors** dialog box.

Clicking on **OK** returns the **Repeated Measures** dialog box of Figure 10.4, where clicking on **Goback** twice returns the **Additional Options** menu. Clicking on **Output statistics...** produces the **Output Statistics** menu of Figure 8.10, where clicking on **Means...** produces the **Effect Selection** menu of Figure 10.6.

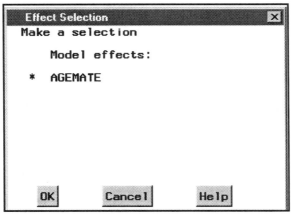

Figure 10.6   **Effect Selection** menu for profile analysis.

AGEMATE is selected so that means for each of the subtests are requested for each group. Clicking on **Goback** twice returns the **Analysis of Variance** dialog box, where clicking on the runner icon produces *Output 10.2.*

Output 10.1   PROFILE ANALYSIS OF SIX WISC SUBTESTS (SELECTED OUTPUT)

```
                          The GLM Procedure

                      Class Level Information

                   Class        Levels      Values

                   AGEMATE           3       1 2 3


                Number of observations      177
```

NOTE: Observations with missing values will not be included in this analysis.   Thus, only 165 observations can be used in this analysis.

Level of AGEMATE	N	-----------INFO----------- Mean	Std Dev	-----------COMP----------- Mean	Std Dev	-----------ARITH---------- Mean	Std Dev
1	45	9.0666667	3.32620450	9.5111111	2.89688094	9.22222222	2.71267135
2	55	10.1818182	3.24374560	10.4545455	2.85331634	8.83636364	2.25062655
3	65	9.3692308	2.54072597	10.1230769	2.88047138	9.13846154	2.49297089

Level of		----------SIMIL----------		-----------VOCAB----------		-----------DIGIT----------	
AGEMATE	N	Mean	Std Dev	Mean	Std Dev	Mean	Std Dev
1	45	9.8666667	3.25855517	10.2888889	3.48126298	8.53333333	2.68497503
2	55	11.2363636	2.96250417	11.4363636	2.78729682	8.98181818	2.52755854
3	65	10.7538462	3.44615170	10.3692308	2.75323237	8.73846154	2.62367183

Repeated Measures Analysis of Variance

Repeated Measures Level Information

| Dependent Variable | INFO | COMP | ARITH | SIMIL | VOCAB | DIGIT |
| Level of SUBTEST | 1 | 2 | 3 | 4 | 5 | 6 |

Manova Test Criteria and Exact F Statistics for the Hypothesis of no SUBTEST Effect
H = Type III SSCP Matrix for SUBTEST
E = Error SSCP Matrix

S=1   M=1.5   N=78

Statistic	Value	F Value	Num DF	Den DF	Pr > F
Wilks' Lambda	0.65163911	16.89	5	158	<.0001
Pillai's Trace	0.34836089	16.89	5	158	<.0001
Hotelling-Lawley Trace	0.53459175	16.89	5	158	<.0001
Roy's Greatest Root	0.53459175	16.89	5	158	<.0001

Manova Test Criteria and F Approximations for the Hypothesis of no SUBTEST*AGEMATE Effect
H = Type III SSCP Matrix for SUBTEST*AGEMATE
E = Error SSCP Matrix

S=2   M=1   N=78

Statistic	Value	F Value	Num DF	Den DF	Pr > F
Wilks' Lambda	0.91551924	1.43	10	316	0.1675
Pillai's Trace	0.08565691	1.42	10	318	0.1688
Hotelling-Lawley Trace	0.09099165	1.43	10	234.27	0.1671
Roy's Greatest Root	0.07351699	2.34	5	159	0.0443

NOTE: F Statistic for Roy's Greatest Root is an upper bound.
NOTE: F Statistic for Wilks' Lambda is exact.

The GLM Procedure
Repeated Measures Analysis of Variance
Tests of Hypotheses for Between Subjects Effects

Source	DF	Type III SS	Mean Square	F Value	Pr > F
AGEMATE	2	90.717224	45.358612	1.69	0.1877
Error	162	4346.933282	26.832921		

Notice that the SUBTEST by AGEMATE interaction (parallelism test) is not statistically significant in the analysis of six subtests, however SUBTEST differences remain.

10.2   DOUBLY MULTIVARIATE ANALYSIS OF REACTION TIME

This example assesses practice effects over four sessions for two target objects: the letter G or a symbol. The two noncommensurate DVs are the (1) slope, and (2) intercept, calculated from reactions times over four angles of rotation.

10.2.1   Evaluation of Assumptions

Section 4.3 of this workbook shows how to find frequency distributions and histograms for the eight DVs (four intercept measures and four slope measures) separately for each target type (GROUP). Section 4.2.3 shows how to find within-groups multivariate outliers using separate multiple regression analyses for each group, and how to evaluate multicollinearity. Sample sizes are equal and ratios of variance for all eight variables are well within acceptable limits.

Homogeneity of regression evaluations for stepdown analysis are not run because there is no straightforward way to create covariates and to run analysis of covariance from the m-matrix transformations that are necessary for doubly multivariate analyses. Therefore, stepdown analysis is impractical in SAS. A reasonable alternative is to report univariate results along with pooled within cell correlations among original DVs.

10.2.2 Doubly Multivariate Analysis of Slope and Intercept

SAS/ASSIST has no provision for specifying m-matrices necessary for running a doubly multivariate analysis. Therefore, a batch file is prepared as per the small sample example of Table 10.14 of *UMS*. The only difference is that means are requested rather than lsmeans, convenient for producing standard deviations (Figure 10.7) as long as there is only one grouping variable.

```
Program Editor - dblmult.sas  PROC GLM running
proc glm data=SASUSER.DBLMULT;
  class GROUP;
  model INTRCPT1 INTRCPT2 INTRCPT3 INTRCPT4 SLOPE1 SLOPE2 SLOPE3 SLOPE4 = GROUP;
/*Test for LEVELS effect */
  manova h=GROUP
     m=INTRCPT1+INTRCPT2+INTRCPT3+INTRCPT4, SLOPE1+SLOPE2+SLOPE3+SLOPE4/summary;
/*Test for FLATNESS effect */
  manova h=intercept
     m=(-3 -1  1  3  0  0  0  0,
         1 -1 -1  1  0  0  0  0,
        -1  3 -3  1  0  0  0  0,
         0  0  0  0 -3 -1  1  3,
         0  0  0  0  1 -1 -1  1,
         0  0  0  0 -1  3 -3  1 )/summary;
/*Test for PARALLELISM effect */
  manova h=GROUP
     m=(-3 -1  1  3  0  0  0  0,
         1 -1 -1  1  0  0  0  0,
        -1  3 -3  1  0  0  0  0,
         0  0  0  0 -3 -1  1  3,
         0  0  0  0  1 -1 -1  1,
         0  0  0  0 -1  3 -3  1 )/summary;
  means GROUP;
run;
```

Figure 10.7   Batch file for doubly multivariate analysis.

Clicking on the runner icon produces *Output 10.2.*

Output 10.2   DOUBLY MULTIVARIATE ANALYSIS OF SLOPE AND INTERCEPT, PARTIAL
OUTPUT.

The GLM Procedure

Class Level Information

Class	Levels	Values
GROUP	2	1 2

Number of observations   20

The GLM Procedure
Multivariate Analysis of Variance

M Matrix Describing Transformed Variables

	INTRCPT1	INTRCPT2	INTRCPT3	INTRCPT4
MVAR1	1	1	1	1
MVAR2	0	0	0	0

128

M Matrix Describing Transformed Variables

	SLOPE1	SLOPE2	SLOPE3	SLOPE4
MVAR1	0	0	0	0
MVAR2	1	1	1	1

MANOVA Test Criteria and Exact F Statistics for the Hypothesis of No Overall GROUP Effect
on the Variables Defined by the M Matrix Transformation
H = Type III SSCP Matrix for GROUP
E = Error SSCP Matrix

S=1   M=0   N=7.5

Statistic	Value	F Value	Num DF	Den DF	Pr > F
Wilks' Lambda	0.26878232	23.12	2	17	<.0001
Pillai's Trace	0.73121768	23.12	2	17	<.0001
Hotelling-Lawley Trace	2.72048285	23.12	2	17	<.0001
Roy's Greatest Root	2.72048285	23.12	2	17	<.0001

The GLM Procedure
Multivariate Analysis of Va nce

Dependent Variable: MVAR1

Source	DF	Type III SS	Mean Square	F Value	Pr > F
GROUP	1	749232.0500	749232.0500	44.68	<.0001
Error	18	301872.5000	16770.6944		

Dependent Variable: MVAR2

Source	DF	Type III SS	Mean Square	F Value	Pr > F
GROUP	1	128480.450	128480.450	0.59	0.4514
Error	18	3902860.500	216825.583		

M Matrix Describing Transformed Variables

	INTRCPT1	INTRCPT2	INTRCPT3	INTRCPT4
MVAR1	-3	-1	1	3
MVAR2	1	-1	-1	1
MVAR3	-1	3	-3	1
MVAR4	0	0	0	0
MVAR5	0	0	0	0
MVAR6	0	0	0	0

M Matrix Describing Transformed Variables

	SLOPE1	SLOPE2	SLOPE3	SLOPE4
MVAR1	0	0	0	0
MVAR2	0	0	0	0
MVAR3	0	0	0	0
MVAR4	-3	-1	1	3
MVAR5	1	-1	-1	1
MVAR6	-1	3	-3	1

MANOVA Test Criteria and Exact F Statistics for the Hypothesis of No Overall Intercept Effect
on the Variables Defined by the M Matrix Transformation
H = Type III SSCP Matrix for Intercept
E = Error SSCP Matrix

S=1   M=2   N=5.5

Statistic	Value	F Value	Num DF	Den DF	Pr > F
Wilks' Lambda	0.11009160	17.51	6	13	<.0001
Pillai's Trace	0.88990840	17.51	6	13	<.0001
Hotelling-Lawley Trace	8.08334499	17.51	6	13	<.0001
Roy's Greatest Root	8.08334499	17.51	6	13	<.0001

Dependent Variable: MVAR1

Source	DF	Type III SS	Mean Square	F Value	Pr > F
Intercept	1	1176610.050	1176610.050	89.32	<.0001
Error	18	237110.500	13172.806		

Dependent Variable: MVAR2

Source	DF	Type III SS	Mean Square	F Value	Pr > F
Intercept	1	21060.05000	21060.05000	19.68	0.0003
Error	18	19258.50000	1069.91667		

Dependent Variable: MVAR3

Source	DF	Type III SS	Mean Square	F Value	Pr > F
Intercept	1	684.45000	684.45000	0.29	0.5981
Error	18	42784.50000	2376.91667		

Dependent Variable: MVAR4

Source	DF	Type III SS	Mean Square	F Value	Pr > F
Intercept	1	4152338.45	4152338.45	5.52	0.0304
Error	18	13543398.50	752411.03		

Dependent Variable: MVAR5

Source	DF	Type III SS	Mean Square	F Value	Pr > F
Intercept	1	3050.4500	3050.4500	0.08	0.7767
Error	18	662464.1000	36803.5611		

Dependent Variable: MVAR6

Source	DF	Type III SS	Mean Square	F Value	Pr > F
Intercept	1	152950.0500	152950.0500	3.90	0.0638
Error	18	705848.5000	39213.8056		

M Matrix Describing Transformed Variables

	INTRCPT1	INTRCPT2	INTRCPT3	INTRCPT4
MVAR1	-3	-1	1	3
MVAR2	1	-1	-1	1
MVAR3	-1	3	-3	1
MVAR4	0	0	0	0
MVAR5	0	0	0	0
MVAR6	0	0	0	0

M Matrix Describing Transformed Variables

	SLOPE1	SLOPE2	SLOPE3	SLOPE4
MVAR1	0	0	0	0
MVAR2	0	0	0	0
MVAR3	0	0	0	0
MVAR4	-3	-1	1	3
MVAR5	1	-1	-1	1
MVAR6	-1	3	-3	1

MANOVA Test Criteria and Exact F Statistics for the Hypothesis of No Overall GROUP Effect
on the Variables Defined by the M Matrix Transformation
H = Type III SSCP Matrix for GROUP
E = Error SSCP Matrix

S=1   M=2   N=5.5

Statistic	Value	F Value	Num DF	Den DF	Pr > F
Wilks' Lambda	0.17911604	9.93	6	13	0.0003
Pillai's Trace	0.82088396	9.93	6	13	0.0003
Hotelling-Lawley Trace	4.58297288	9.93	6	13	0.0003
Roy's Greatest Root	4.58297288	9.93	6	13	0.0003

Dependent Variable: MVAR1

Source	DF	Type III SS	Mean Square	F Value	Pr > F
GROUP	1	690804.4500	690804.4500	52.44	<.0001
Error	18	237110.5000	13172.8056		

Dependent Variable: MVAR2

Source	DF	Type III SS	Mean Square	F Value	Pr > F
GROUP	1	5346.45000	5346.45000	5.00	0.0383
Error	18	19258.50000	1069.91667		

Dependent Variable: MVAR3

Source	DF	Type III SS	Mean Square	F Value	Pr > F
GROUP	1	1296.05000	1296.05000	0.55	0.4698
Error	18	42784.50000	2376.91667		

Dependent Variable: MVAR4

Source	DF	Type III SS	Mean Square	F Value	Pr > F
GROUP	1	7960.05	7960.05	0.01	0.9192
Error	18	13543398.50	752411.03		

Dependent Variable: MVAR5

Source	DF	Type III SS	Mean Square	F Value	Pr > F
GROUP	1	28350.4500	28350.4500	0.77	0.3917
Error	18	662464.1000	36803.5611		

Dependent Variable: MVAR6

Source	DF	Type III SS	Mean Square	F Value	Pr > F
GROUP	1	20034.4500	20034.4500	0.51	0.4839
Error	18	705848.5000	39213.8056		

Level of GROUP	N	---------INTRCPT1--------- Mean	Std Dev	---------INTRCPT2--------- Mean	Std Dev	---------INTRCPT3--------- Mean	Std Dev
1	10	200.700000	42.2691114	133.900000	46.8103740	90.4000000	30.2515381
2	10	40.800000	49.6494377	24.300000	29.8553922	22.8000000	29.1806633

Level of GROUP	N	---------INTRCPT4--------- Mean	Std Dev	----------SLOPE1---------- Mean	Std Dev	----------SLOPE2---------- Mean	Std Dev
1	10	72.4000000	25.9965810	642.500000	129.859112	581.100000	97.793944
2	10	22.4000000	26.4289404	654.600000	375.511858	647.500000	153.904191

| Level of | | ------------SLOPE3----------- | | ------------SLOPE4----------- | |
GROUP	N	Mean	Std Dev	Mean	Std Dev
1	10	516.800000	65.0176045	505.400000	67.3369636
2	10	568.200000	59.8512972	535.800000	50.1061096

Tables labeled M Matrix Describing Transformed Variables show the created variables and their labels. For example, the first such table shows that MVAR1 is the created intercept DV (all of the individual INTRCPT variables are coded 1) and MVAR2 is the created slope DV (all of the individual SLOPE variables are coded 1).

Looking at the parallelism test first (the last multivariate table) we see a significant effect, $F(6, 13) = 9.93$, $\eta^2 = 1 - $ Wilks' Lambda $= .82$. Therefore, only this test is interpreted. The M Matrix Describing Transformed Variables for this effect shows that MVAR1 is the linear trend for intercept, MVAR2 is the quadratic trend for intercept, MVAR3 is the cubic trend for intercept, MVAR4 is the linear trend for slope, and so on. With $\alpha = .0083$ to compensate for inflated Type I error rate, only the linear trend of intercept is statistically reliable.

Partial η^2 is calculated as for the example in *UMS*. Although all sums of squares are double the values shown in Table 10.22 of *UMS*, proportion of variance remains the same:

$$\text{partial } \eta^2 = \frac{690804.45}{690804.45 + 237110.50} = .74$$

Pooled within-cell correlations are found by running a simple repeated measures ANOVA using the whole set of DVs: INTRCPT1 through SLOPE4. SAS/ASSIST is unable to handle the eight DVs, therefore a batch file is run. PRINTE is the instruction that requests the desired matrix.

```
Program Editor - [Untitled]  PROC GLM running
proc glm data=SASUSER.DBLMULT;
    class GROUP;
    model INTRCPT1 INTRCPT2 INTRCPT3 INTRCPT4 SLOPE1 SLOPE2 SLOPE3 SLOPE4 = GROUP ;
    repeated DVs 8 /PRINTE ;
run;
```

Figure 10.8   Batch file for pooled within-cell correlations.

133

Clicking on the runner icon produces *Output 10.3*.

Output 10.3   POOLED WITHIN-CELL CORRELATIONS AMONG ORIGINAL DVs.

The GLM Procedure
Repeated Measures Analysis of Variance

Repeated Measures Level Information

Dependent Variable	INTRCPT1	INTRCPT2	INTRCPT3	INTRCPT4	SLOPE1	SLOPE2	SLOPE3	SLOPE4
Level of DVs	1	2	3	4	5	6	7	8

Partial Correlation Coefficients from the Error SSCP Matrix / Prob > |r|

DF = 18	INTRCPT1	INTRCPT2	INTRCPT3	INTRCPT4	SLOPE1	SLOPE2	SLOPE3	SLOPE4
INTRCPT1	1.000000	0.742959	0.706584	0.639885	0.084502	0.052549	0.092301	0.018816
		0.0003	0.0007	0.0032	0.7309	0.8308	0.7070	0.9391
INTRCPT2	0.742959	1.000000	0.915263	0.845713	0.204540	0.207412	0.130219	0.017668
	0.0003		<.0001	<.0001	0.4009	0.3942	0.5952	0.9428
INTRCPT3	0.706584	0.915263	1.000000	0.952046	0.195504	0.266249	0.087773	-0.012000
	0.0007	<.0001		<.0001	0.4225	0.2705	0.7209	0.9611
INTRCPT4	0.639885	0.845713	0.952046	1.000000	0.308194	0.271530	0.076175	-0.055556
	0.0032	<.0001	<.0001		0.1992	0.2608	0.7566	0.8213
SLOPE1	0.084502	0.204540	0.195504	0.308194	1.000000	0.753809	0.516688	0.321691
	0.7309	0.4009	0.4225	0.1992		0.0002	0.0235	0.1793
SLOPE2	0.052549	0.207412	0.266249	0.271530	0.753809	1.000000	0.812813	0.672703
	0.8308	0.3942	0.2705	0.2608	0.0002		<.0001	0.0016
SLOPE3	0.092301	0.130219	0.087773	0.076175	0.516688	0.812813	1.000000	0.938076
	0.7070	0.5952	0.7209	0.7566	0.0235	<.0001		<.0001
SLOPE4	0.018816	0.017668	-0.012000	-0.055556	0.321691	0.672703	0.938076	1.000000
	0.9391	0.9428	0.9611	0.8213	0.1793	0.0016	<.0001	

Correlations among intercept variables and among slope variables are substantial, however, correlations between intercept and slope variables are not statistically reliable. Therefore, we can feel comfortable in reporting univariate rather than stepdown results for the trend analyses.

134

Chapter 11. Discriminant Function Analysis

This chapter demonstrates direct discriminant function analysis with cross-validation and group contrasts using SAS for Windows, for the complete example of Chapter 11 in *UMS*. The file to use is DISCRIM.SAS7BDAT.

This example evaluates prediction of work status and satisfaction with it (WORKSTAT) by four attitudinal variables: attitudes toward housework (ATTHOUSE), attitudes toward current marital status (ATTMAR), attitudes toward the role of women (ATTROLE), and locus of control (CONTROL). Groups are formed by women who are (1) currently employed–WORKING, (2) role-satisfied housewives–HAPHOUSE, or (3) role-dissatisfied housewives–UNHOUSE.

11.1   EVALUATION OF ASSUMPTIONS

Data screening for grouped data through frequencies and histograms is described in Section 4.2 and is done for each WORKSTAT group. Section 4.2.3 demonstrates a search for multivariate outliers and evaluation of multicollinearity using separate regressions for each group. Deletion of the two cases with extreme values on ATTHOUSE is demonstrated in Section 4.1.2. After deletion, 456 of the original 465 cases remain in the data file.

Homogeneity of variance-covariance matrices is tested in SAS through PROC DISCRIM using batch processing. Figure 11.2 shows the instruction file in the **Program Editor** that provides the test. Note that most output has been suppressed here to limit the output. The instruction to produce the test of homogeneity of variance-covariance matrices is pool=test.

```
proc discrim data=SASUSER.DISCRIM short noclassify
        pool=test;
    class workstat;
    var CONTROL ATTMAR ATTROLE ATTHOUSE;
    priors proportional;
        where CASESEQ^=346 and CASESEQ^=407;
run;
```

Figure 11.1   Batch file to test homogeneity of variance-
                covariance matrices.

Clicking on the runner icon on the toolbar produces *Output 11.1*.

Output 11.1   TEST OF HOMOGENEITY OF VARIANCE-COVARIANCE MATRICES IN PROC
                    DISCRIM.

The DISCRIM Procedure

Observations	456	DF Total	455
Variables	4	DF Within Classes	453
Classes	3	DF Between Classes	2

Class Level Information

WORKSTAT	Variable Name	Frequency	Weight	Proportion	Prior Probability
1	_1	239	239.0000	0.524123	0.524123
2	_2	136	136.0000	0.298246	0.298246
3	_3	81	81.0000	0.177632	0.177632

Test of Homogeneity of Within Covariance Matrices

Notation: K   = Number of Groups

          P   = Number of Variables

          N   = Total Number of Observations - Number of Groups

          N(i) = Number of Observations in the i'th Group - 1

$$V = \frac{\prod |Within\ SS\ Matrix(i)|^{N(i)/2}}{|Pooled\ SS\ Matrix|^{N/2}}$$

136

```
                            _            _    2
                           |    1      1 | 2P + 3P - 1
       RHO   = 1.0 -  | SUM -----  -  --- | -------------
                           |_   N(i)      N _|  6(P+1)(K-1)


       DF    = .5(K-1)P(P+1)

                                                    _               _
                                                   |     PN/2         |
                                                   |   N         V    |
       Under the null hypothesis:       -2 RHO ln  | ----------------- |
                                                   |    __      PN(i)/2 |
                                                   |_   ||  N(i)      _|
```

is distributed approximately as Chi-Square(DF).

```
          Chi-Square         DF      Pr > ChiSq

          50.753826          20        0.0002
```

Since the Chi-Square value is significant at the 0.1 level, the within covariance
matrices will be used in the discriminant function.
Reference: Morrison, D.F. (1976) Multivariate Statistical Methods
p252.

Note that this test shows significant heterogeneity of variance-covariance matrices. The

program uses separate matrices in the classification phase of discriminant function analysis if

pool=test is specified and the test shows significant heterogeneity.

11.2   DIRECT DISCRIMINANT FUNCTION ANALYSIS

11.2.1 Main Analysis

A multivariate test of the significance of the difference among the three WORKSTAT groups

may be performed by following the SAS/ASSIST procedures for MANOVA in Chapter 9 of this

workbook, with WORKSTAT as the IV and CONTROL, ATTMAR, ATTROLE, and

ATTHOUSE as DVs. The multivariate test based on Wilks' Lambda matches that of Table

11.15 in *Using Multivariate Statistics*. This procedure is especially useful for assessing contrasts among groups, as illustrated in Section 11.2.3 in this workbook.

However, this procedure provides no classification information, nor are discriminant function coefficients available. To get these values, a full discriminant function analysis is required, which is done through batch processing rather than SAS/ASSIST. Figure 11.2 shows the batch file to request the full discriminant function analysis.

```
proc discrim data=SASUSER.DISCRIM anova manova pcorr can
        crossvalidate;
    class workstat;
    var CONTROL ATTMAR ATTROLE ATTHOUSE;
    priors proportional;
        where CASESEQ^=346 and CASESEQ^=407;
run;
```

Figure 11.2   Instruction file for discriminant function analysis.

The anova and manova instructions request univariate statistics on group differences separately for each of the variables and a multivariate test for the difference among groups. Pcorr requests the pooled within-groups correlation matrix, and crossvalidate requests jackknifed classification. The priors proportional instruction specifies prior probabilities for classification proportional to sample sizes. Note that the pool=test instruction has been omitted in order to match output as closely as possible with that of Section 11.8 in *UMS*. A later run shows the classification results produced by using separate variance-covariance matrices. Clicking on the runner icon on the toolbar produces *Output 11.2*.

Output 11.2   DISCRIMINANT FUNCTION ANALYSIS OF FOUR ATTITUDINAL VARIABLES.

The DISCRIM Procedure

Observations	456	DF Total	455
Variables	4	DF Within Classes	453
Classes	3	DF Between Classes	2

Class Level Information

WORKSTAT	Variable Name	Frequency	Weight	Proportion	Prior Probability
1	_1	239	239.0000	0.524123	0.524123
2	_2	136	136.0000	0.298246	0.298246
3	_3	81	81.0000	0.177632	0.177632

Pooled Within-Class Correlation Coefficients / Pr > |r|

Variable	CONTROL	ATTMAR	ATTROLE	ATTHOUSE
CONTROL	1.00000	0.17169	0.00912	0.15500
Locus-of-control		0.0002	0.8463	0.0009
ATTMAR	0.17169	1.00000	-0.07010	0.28229
Attitude toward current marital status	0.0002		0.1359	<.0001
ATTROLE	0.00912	-0.07010	1.00000	-0.29145
Attitudes toward role of women	0.8463	0.1359		<.0001
ATTHOUSE	0.15500	0.28229	-0.29145	1.00000
Attitudes toward housework	0.0009	<.0001	<.0001	

Pooled Covariance Matrix Information

Covariance Matrix Rank	Natural Log of the Determinant of the Covariance Matrix
4	11.14797

Pairwise Generalized Squared Distances Between Groups

$$D^2(i|j) = (\bar{X}_i - \bar{X}_j)' \; COV^{-1} \; (\bar{X}_i - \bar{X}_j) - 2 \ln PRIOR_j$$

Generalized Squared Distance to WORKSTAT

From WORKSTAT	1	2	3
1	1.29206	2.77142	3.73057
2	1.64381	2.41968	4.03490
3	1.56654	2.99849	3.45609

Univariate Test Statistics

F Statistics,   Num DF=2,   Den DF=453

Total   Pooled   Between

139

Variable	Label	Standard Deviation	Standard Deviation	Standard Deviation	R-Square	R-Square / (1-RSq)	F Value	Pr > F
CONTROL	Locus-of-control	1.2679	1.2625	0.1761	0.0129	0.0131	2.96	0.0530
ATTMAR	Attitude toward current marital status	8.5287	8.3683	2.1254	0.0415	0.0433	9.81	<.0001
ATTROLE	Attitudes toward role of women	6.7590	6.6115	1.7996	0.0474	0.0497	11.26	<.0001
ATTHOUSE	Attitudes toward housework	4.2786	4.2061	1.0184	0.0379	0.0393	8.91	0.0002

Multivariate Statistics and F Approximations

S=2   M=0.5   N=224

Statistic	Value	F Value	Num DF	Den DF	Pr > F
Wilks' Lambda	0.89715033	6.27	8	900	<.0001
Pillai's Trace	0.10527259	6.26	8	902	<.0001
Hotelling-Lawley Trace	0.11193972	6.29	8	640.54	<.0001
Roy's Greatest Root	0.07675307	8.65	4	451	<.0001

NOTE: F Statistic for Roy's Greatest Root is an upper bound.
NOTE: F Statistic for Wilks' Lambda is exact.

Canonical Discriminant Analysis

	Canonical Correlation	Adjusted Canonical Correlation	Approximate Standard Error	Squared Canonical Correlation
1	0.266987	0.245497	0.043539	0.071282
2	0.184365	0.182794	0.045287	0.033991

Eigenvalues of Inv(E)*H = CanRsq/(1-CanRsq)

Test of HO: The canonical correlations in the current row and all that follow are zero

	Eigenvalue	Difference	Proportion	Cumulative	Likelihood Ratio	Approximate F Value	Num DF	Den DF	Pr > F
1	0.0768	0.0416	0.6857	0.6857	0.89715033	6.27	8	900	<.0001
2	0.0352		0.3143	1.0000	0.96600937	5.29	3	451	0.0014

Canonical Discriminant Analysis

Total Canonical Structure

Variable	Label	Can1	Can2
CONTROL	Locus-of-control	0.290398	0.449773
ATTMAR	Attitude toward current marital status	0.729892	0.321735
ATTROLE	Attitudes toward role of women	-0.647428	0.717212
ATTHOUSE	Attitudes toward housework	0.691567	0.332648

Between Canonical Structure

Variable	Label	Can1	Can2
CONTROL	Locus-of-control	0.682968	0.730448
ATTMAR	Attitude toward current marital status	0.956663	0.291198
ATTROLE	Attitudes toward role of women	-0.794256	0.607584
ATTHOUSE	Attitudes toward housework	0.949018	0.315221

Pooled Within Canonical Structure

Variable	Label	Can1	Can2
CONTROL	Locus-of-control	0.281678	0.444939
ATTMAR	Attitude toward current marital status	0.718461	0.322992
ATTROLE	Attitudes toward role of women	-0.639249	0.722228
ATTHOUSE	Attitudes toward housework	0.679447	0.333315

Total-Sample Standardized Canonical Coefficients

Variable	Label	Can1	Can2
CONTROL	Locus-of-control	0.1355542259	0.3306926502
ATTMAR	Attitude toward current marital status	0.5708175534	0.1950633792
ATTROLE	Attitudes toward role of women	-.5087431038	0.8928225980
ATTHOUSE	Attitudes toward housework	0.3615113068	0.4911027502

Pooled Within-Class Standardized Canonical Coefficients

Variable	Label	Can1	Can2
CONTROL	Locus-of-control	0.1349748946	0.3292793367
ATTMAR	Attitude toward current marital status	0.5600818048	0.1913946913
ATTROLE	Attitudes toward role of women	-.4976440156	0.8733441682
ATTHOUSE	Attitudes toward housework	0.3553851001	0.4827804739

Raw Canonical Coefficients

Variable	Label	Can1	Can2
CONTROL	Locus-of-control	0.1069083420	0.2608093013
ATTMAR	Attitude toward current marital status	0.0669289324	0.0228713774
ATTROLE	Attitudes toward role of women	-.0752695186	0.1320948170
ATTHOUSE	Attitudes toward housework	0.0844931701	0.1147815501

Class Means on Canonical Variables

WORKSTAT	Can1	Can2
1	0.1407162321	-.1505321835

```
        2      -.4160079128      0.0539321812
        3      0.2832826750      0.3536100644
```

Linear Discriminant Function

$$\text{Constant}_j = -.5 \ \bar{X}'_j \ \text{COV}^{-1} \ \bar{X}_j + \ln \text{PRIOR}_j \qquad \text{Coefficient Vector} = \text{COV}^{-1} \ \bar{X}_j$$

Linear Discriminant Function for WORKSTAT

Variable	Label	1	2	3
Constant		-50.30083	-52.00881	-56.55485
CONTROL	Locus-of-control	3.22293	3.21674	3.36966
ATTMAR	Attitude toward current marital status	0.07664	0.04406	0.09771
ATTROLE	Attitudes toward role of women	1.08148	1.15040	1.13735
ATTHOUSE	Attitudes toward housework	1.64843	1.62485	1.71834

Classification Summary for Calibration Data: SASUSER.DISCRIM
Resubstitution Summary using Linear Discriminant Function

Generalized Squared Distance Function

$$D^2_j(X) = (X-\bar{X}_j)' \ \text{COV}^{-1} \ (X-\bar{X}_j) - 2 \ln \text{PRIOR}_j$$

Posterior Probability of Membership in Each WORKSTAT

$$\Pr(j|X) = \exp(-.5 \ D^2_j(X)) \ / \ \text{SUM}_k \ \exp(-.5 \ D^2_k(X))$$

Number of Observations and Percent Classified into WORKSTAT

From WORKSTAT	1	2	3	Total
1	206	31	2	239
	86.19	12.97	0.84	100.00
2	97	37	2	136
	71.32	27.21	1.47	100.00
3	66	11	4	81
	81.48	13.58	4.94	100.00
Total	369	79	8	456
	80.92	17.32	1.75	100.00
Priors	0.52412	0.29825	0.17763	

142

Error Count Estimates for WORKSTAT

	1	2	3	Total
Rate	0.1381	0.7279	0.9506	0.4583
Priors	0.5241	0.2982	0.1776	

The DISCRIM Procedure
Classification Summary for Calibration Data: SASUSER.DISCRIM
Cross-validation Summary using Linear Discriminant Function

Generalized Squared Distance Function

$$D_j^2(X) = (X - \bar{X}_{(X)j})' \, COV_{(X)}^{-1} \, (X - \bar{X}_{(X)j}) - 2 \ln PRIOR_j$$

Posterior Probability of Membership in Each WORKSTAT

$$Pr(j|X) = \exp(-.5 \, D_j^2(X)) \, / \, SUM_k \, \exp(-.5 \, D_k^2(X))$$

Number of Observations and Percent Classified into WORKSTAT

From WORKSTAT	1	2	3	Total
1	205	32	2	239
	85.77	13.39	0.84	100.00
2	98	36	2	136
	72.06	26.47	1.47	100.00
3	66	11	4	81
	81.48	13.58	4.94	100.00
Total	369	79	8	456
	80.92	17.32	1.75	100.00
Priors	0.52412	0.29825	0.17763	

Error Count Estimates for WORKSTAT

	1	2	3	Total
Rate	0.1423	0.7353	0.9506	0.4627
Priors	0.5241	0.2982	0.1776	

The `Pooled Within-Class Correlation Coefficients` show the relationship among variables pooled within groups. The `univariate` and `multivariate` test statistics match those of Section 11.8 in *UMS*. The `Canonical Correlations`, `Eigenvalues`, and `Cumulative Proportion` match those of Table 11.10 in *UMS*. `Adjusted Canonical Correlations` and their standard errors also are shown. Peel-off significance tests are shown as `Approximate F Value` and correspond to the χ^2 tests of Table 11.12. The first (`F = 6.27`) tests the significance of both canonical functions; the second tests only the last canonical function, after the first is removed. Then several tables are shown indicating relationships between variables and canonical variates. The one of greatest interest is the loading matrix, labeled `Pooled Canonical Structure`. Group centroids are labeled `Class Means on Canonical Variables`. Classification functions appear in the output labeled `Linear Discriminant Function`. Note that all except the constants exactly match those in *UMS*. Then two classification tables are shown, first without and then with jackknifing (labeled `Cross-validation Summary...`). These do not exactly match the classification tables in Table 11.10 of *UMS*, however the overall error rates differ little.

Recall from Section 11.1 above, however, that the test of homogeneity of variance-covariance matrices suggested the desirability of using separate matrices rather than the pooled one. If pool=test is retained in the instructions, all output remains the same except for classification tables. *Output 11.3* shows the resulting classification tables.

Output 11.3   RESULTS OF CLASSIFICATION WITH SEPARATE VARIANCE-COVARIANCES MATRICES.

```
                     The DISCRIM Procedure
        Classification Summary for Calibration Data: SASUSER.DISCRIM
           Resubstitution Summary using Quadratic Discriminant Function

                    Generalized Squared Distance Function

    2              _         -1   _
   D (X) = (X-X )' COV   (X-X ) + ln |COV | - 2 ln PRIOR
    j           j     j   j            j              j

         Posterior Probability of Membership in Each WORKSTAT

                             2                      2
        Pr(j|X) = exp(-.5 D (X)) / SUM exp(-.5 D (X))
```

144

Number of Observations and Percent Classified into WORKSTAT

From WORKSTAT	1	2	3	Total
1	184 76.99	48 20.08	7 2.93	239 100.00
2	73 53.68	59 43.38	4 2.94	136 100.00
3	59 72.84	12 14.81	10 12.35	81 100.00
Total	316 69.30	119 26.10	21 4.61	456 100.00
Priors	0.52412	0.29825	0.17763	

Error Count Estimates for WORKSTAT

	1	2	3	Total
Rate	0.2301	0.5662	0.8765	0.4452
Priors	0.5241	0.2982	0.1776	

Classification Summary for Calibration Data: SASUSER.DISCRIM
Cross-validation Summary using Quadratic Discriminant Function

Generalized Squared Distance Function

$$D_j^2(X) = (X-\bar{X}_{(X)j})' \, COV_{(X)j}^{-1} \, (X-\bar{X}_{(X)j}) + \ln |COV_{(X)j}| - 2 \ln PRIOR_j$$

Posterior Probability of Membership in Each WORKSTAT

$$Pr(j|X) = \exp(-.5\, D_j^2(X)) \; / \; \mathrm{SUM}_k \, \exp(-.5\, D_k^2(X))$$

Number of Observations and Percent Classified into WORKSTAT

From WORKSTAT	1	2	3	Total
1	179 74.90	50 20.92	10 4.18	239 100.00
2	78 57.35	53 38.97	5 3.68	136 100.00

145

		3	60	13	8	81
			74.07	16.05	9.88	100.00
	Total		317	116	23	456
			69.52	25.44	5.04	100.00
	Priors		0.52412	0.29825	0.17763	

Error Count Estimates for WORKSTAT

	1	2	3	Total
Rate	0.2510	0.6103	0.9012	0.4737
Priors	0.5241	0.2982	0.1776	

The overall error rate is reduced from 45.8% to 44.5% with the use of separate variance-covariance matrices in classification without jackknifing. However, with jackknifing, the use of separate variance-covariance matrices slightly increases the error rate.

11.2.2 Cross-validation of Classification of Cases

PROC DISCRIM has no direct procedure of forming and using a cross-validation sample. Instead, other procedures must be used to split the file into the "training" cases, used to develop (calibrate) the classification equations, and the "testing" cases, used to validate the classification.

First a new data set is created: data SASUSER.DISCRIMX. The original data set is identified as set SASUSER.DISCRIM. Then outliers and cases with missing data are omitted. Finally, a variable is created on which to split the data set, here called TEST1, which is set to zero, and then changed to 1 for 25% of the cases. This requires an if...then statement, unavailable in SAS/ASSIST. The batch file to accomplish this appears in Figure 11.3. Clicking on the runner icon on the toolbar creates the "random sample" variable.

```
data SASUSER.DISCRIMX;
  set SASUSER.DISCRIM;
  if atthouse=2 or atthouse = . or attmar = . or attrole = .
    or control=. then delete;
  text1=0;
  if uniform(11738) <= .25 then text1=1;
run;
```

Figure 11.3   Batch file to create 25% random sample of cases.

146

Then an additional two files are created on the basis of TEST1 with set SASUSER.DISCRIMX: a calibration (training) file, through data SASUSER.DISCTRNG, and a cross-validation (test) file through data SASUSER.DISCTEST. The batch file to accomplish this appears in Figure 11.4.

```
data SASUSER.DISCTRNG;
  set SASUSER.DISCRIMX;
  where text1=0;
data SASUSER.DISCTEST;
  set SASUSER.DISCRIMX;
  where text1=1;
run;
```

Figure 11.4   Batch file to create separate data sets for cross-validation of cases.

Clicking on the runner icon on the toolbar creates the two data sets. Finally, the batch file in Figure 11.5 runs a discriminant function on the training file, saves the calibration information in a file called INFO, and then applies the calibration information to the test file.

```
proc discrim data=SASUSER.DISCTRNG outstat=INFO;
  class WORKSTAT;
  var CONTROL ATTMAR ATTROLE ATTHOUSE;
  priors proportional;
run;
proc discrim data=INFO testdata=SASUSER.DISCTEST;
  class WORKSTAT;
  var CONTROL ATTMAR ATTROLE ATTHOUSE;
  priors proportional;
run;
```

Figure 11.5   Batch file for running cross-validation of classification of cases in DISCRIM.

Clicking on the runner icon on the toolbar produces *Output 11.4*.

The DISCRIM Procedure

Observations	339	DF Total	338
Variables	4	DF Within Classes	336
Classes	3	DF Between Classes	2

Linear Discriminant Function

$$\text{Constant}_j = -.5 \; \bar{X}'_j \; COV^{-1} \; \bar{X}_j + \ln PRIOR_j \qquad \text{Coefficient Vector} = COV^{-1} \; \bar{X}_j$$

Linear Discriminant Function for WORKSTAT

Variable	Label	1	2	3
Constant		-48.65702	-51.22158	-56.09254
CONTROL	Locus-of-control	3.42872	3.40426	3.63630
ATTMAR	Attitude toward current marital status	0.03338	0.01322	0.07100
ATTROLE	Attitudes toward role of women	1.06710	1.14970	1.13508
ATTHOUSE	Attitudes toward housework	1.54289	1.53209	1.60957

The DISCRIM Procedure
Classification Summary for Calibration Data: SASUSER.DISCTRNG
Resubstitution Summary using Linear Discriminant Function

Generalized Squared Distance Function

$$D^2_j(X) = (X - \bar{X}_j)' \; COV^{-1} \; (X - \bar{X}_j) - 2 \ln PRIOR_j$$

Posterior Probability of Membership in Each WORKSTAT

$$Pr(j|X) = \exp(-.5 \; D^2_j(X)) \; / \; \underset{k}{SUM} \; \exp(-.5 \; D^2_k(X))$$

148

Number of Observations and Percent Classified into WORKSTAT

From WORKSTAT	1	2	3	Total
1	150 85.71	22 12.57	3 1.71	175 100.00
2	67 63.21	34 32.08	5 4.72	106 100.00
3	42 72.41	10 17.24	6 10.34	58 100.00
Total	259 76.40	66 19.47	14 4.13	339 100.00
Priors	0.51622	0.31268	0.17109	

Error Count Estimates for WORKSTAT

	1	2	3	Total
Rate	0.1429	0.6792	0.8966	0.4395
Priors	0.5162	0.3127	0.1711	

Classification Summary for Test Data: SASUSER.DISCTEST
Classification Summary using Linear Discriminant Function

Generalized Squared Distance Function

$$D_j^2(X) = (X-\bar{X}_j)' \, COV^{-1} \, (X-\bar{X}_j) - 2 \ln PRIOR_j$$

Posterior Probability of Membership in Each WORKSTAT

$$Pr(j|X) = \exp(-.5\, D_j^2(X)) \, / \, SUM_k \exp(-.5\, D_k^2(X))$$

149

Number of Observations and Percent Classified into WORKSTAT

From WORKSTAT	1	2	3	Total
1	50	11	3	64
	78.13	17.19	4.69	100.00
2	19	11	0	30
	63.33	36.67	0.00	100.00
3	18	3	2	23
	78.26	13.04	8.70	100.00
Total	87	25	5	117
	74.36	21.37	4.27	100.00
Priors	0.51622	0.31268	0.17109	

Error Count Estimates for WORKSTAT

	1	2	3	Total
Rate	0.2188	0.6333	0.9130	0.4672
Priors	0.5162	0.3127	0.1711	

The classification functions as well as the results look quite different from those produced in *UMS*, not surprising considering this is a different random sample.

11.2.3 Contrasts among Groups

PROC DISCRIM has no contrast procedure, nor does it provide F or t ratios for predictor variables adjusted for all other variables. However, the information is available using contrasts with separate analyses of covariance for each variable in MANOVA through SAS/ASSIST. In each analysis of covariance, the variable of interest is declared the DV and the remaining variables are declared covariates. The process is demonstrated for ATTHOUSE, in a run that contrasts the WORKING group with HAPHOUSE and UNHOUSE groups.

Follow the instructions for analysis of covariance, Section 8.2.1, with SASUSER.DISCRIM as the **Table:**, ATTHOUSE as the **Dependent:** variable, and CONTROL, ATTMAR, and ATTROLE as the covariates and WORKSTAT as the **Classification:** variable (Figures 8.3 through 8.7).

Then click on **Subset data:** in the **SAS/ASSIST: Analysis of Variance** dialog box and delete outliers on ATTHOUSE as per procedures in Figures 4.21 through 4.22. The **Analysis of Variance** dialog box will look like Figure 11.6.

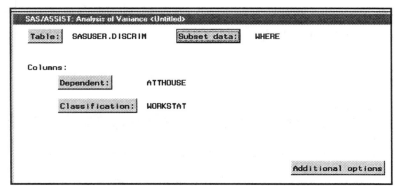

Figure 11.6   **Analysis of Variance** dialog box for contrasts in
                discriminant function analysis.

Clicking on the **Additional options** button, and then **Model hypotheses...** produces the **Model Hypotheses**
menu of Figure 11.7.

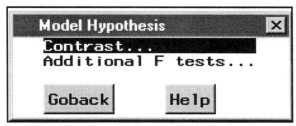

Figure 11.7   **Model Hypothesis** menu.

Clicking on **Contrast...** produces the **Contrast** dialog box of Figure 11.8.

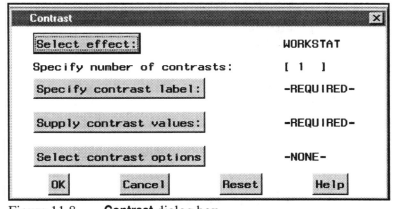

Figure 11.8   **Contrast** dialog box.

151

WORKSTAT is selected from a menu after clicking on **Select effect:**. Clicking **Specify contrast label:** permits typing a contrast label into the **Contrast Label** dialog box, as seen in Figure 11.9.

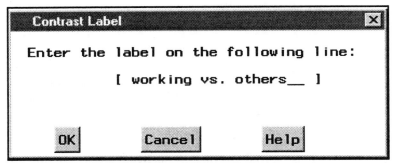

Figure 11.9   **Contrast Label** dialog box.

Clicking on **OK** returns the **Contrast** dialog box, where clicking on **Supply contrast values:** produces the **Contrast Values** dialog box of Figure 11.10.

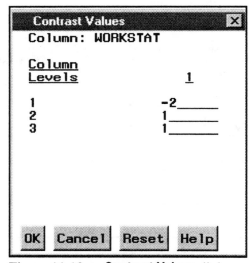

Figure 11.10   **Contrast Values** dialog box.

Coefficients are entered for the three WORKSTAT groups, and clicking on **OK** again returns the **Contrast** dialog box. Clicking on **OK** and then **Goback** twice returns the main **SAS/ASSIST: Analysis of Variance** dialog box, where clicking on the runner icon produces *Output 11.3*.

Output 11.3   CONTRAST BETWEEN WORKING GROUP AND OTHER TWO GROUPS FOR ATTHOUSE. SELECTED OUTPUT.

The GLM Procedure

Class Level Information

Class	Levels	Values
WORKSTAT	3	1 2 3

Number of observations   463

Contrast	DF	Contrast SS	Mean Square	F Value	Pr > F
working vs. others	1	0.74345428	0.74345428	0.04	0.8370

Additional runs are required for the remaining predictor variables (ATTMAR ATTROLE, and CONTROL) and for the other two contrasts (HAPHOUSE vs. the other two groups, and UNHOUSE vs. the other two groups).

153

Chapter 12. Logistic Regression

This chapter demonstrates direct logistic regression with two-category outcome using SAS for Windows, for the complete example of Chapter 12, *Using Multivariate Statistics*. Three-category unordered outcomes are not directly analyzable through SAS: the program assumes that multiple-category outcomes are ordered. However, the analysis of Section 12.7.3 of *UMS* is approximated by separate runs for pairs of work status groups. The file to use is LOGREGCC.SAS7BDAT. This file includes imputed data from SPSS MVA as there is no facility within SAS for EM imputation.

The two-category example evaluates prediction of work status: whether a woman is employed outside the home for more than 20 hours per week. Predictor variables are attitudes toward housework (ATTHOUSE), attitude toward current marital status (ATTMAR), attitude toward role of women (ATTROLE) and locus of control (CONTROL). The three-category example evaluates prediction of the three levels of work status analyzed in the complete example discriminant analysis of Chapter 11: WORKING, HAPHOUSE, and UNHOUSE.

12.1   EVALUATION OF ASSUMPTIONS

The procedure for evaluating expected frequencies follows that of Section 7.1. The requirements regarding expected frequencies are met, as noted in *UMS*.

12.2   DIRECT LOGISTIC REGRESSION WITH TWO-CATEGORY OUTCOME

Data first need to be recoded into two workstat groups, 0 for working women and 1 for the other two groups. Recall that SAS solves logistic regression equations in terms of the group coded 0. This is accomplished through the instructions in the batch file of Figure 12.1.

```
data SASUSER.LOGREG;
  set SASUSER.LOGREGCC;
  if WORKSTAT = 1 then WORKSTAT = 0;
  if WORKSTAT = 3 or WORKSTAT = 2 then WORKSTAT = 1;
run;
```

Figure 12.1   Batch file to recode WORKSTAT into two
                 groups.

Clicking on the runner icon on the toolbar creates the new file, LOGREG, which contains the recoded WORKSTAT variable.

Interactions between continuous variables and their natural logarithms are most easily produced through a batch file as per Figure 12.2. (**Interactive Data Analysis** may be used to create the logarithmically transformed variable but not to form the interaction.) The transformed variables are added to the data set, which is saved as LOGREGIN.SD2.

```
data SASUSER.LOGREGIN;
    set SASUSER.LOGREG;
    LIN_CTRL=LOG(CONTROL)*CONTROL;
    LIN_ATMR=LOG(ATTMAR)*ATTMAR;
    LIN_ATRL=LOG(ATTROLE)*ATTROLE;
    LIN_ATHS=LOG(ATTHOUSE)*ATTHOUSE;
run;
```

Figure 12.2   Syntax to create interactions between continuous predictors and their natural logarithms.

A two-category direct logistic regression analysis is performed with the four original continuous variables and four interactions as predictors, using the new data set which also has recoded values for WORKSTAT. From the **SAS/ASSIST: WorkPlace** window, choosing

> **Data Analysis**
>   > **Regression**
>   > **Logistic...**

produces the **Logistic Regression** dialog box of Figure 12.3. After selecting LOGREG as the **Table:**, and clicking on ⊙**One column** for **Response form is:**, WORKSTAT is selected as the **Response:** variable. **Independent:** variables chosen are CONTROL, ATTMAR, ATTHOUSE, and ATTROLE, LIN_CTRL, LIN_ATMR, LIN_ATHS, and LIN_ATRL.

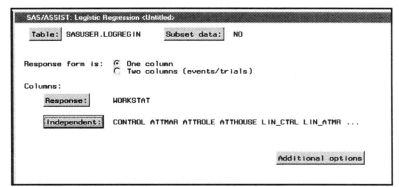

Figure 12.3   **SAS/ASSIST: Logistic Regression** dialog box to test linearity in the logit.

Results are in *Output 12.1.*

Output 12.1   DIRECT LOGISTIC REGRESSION ANALYSIS TO TEST LINEARITY OF THE LOGIT.

The LOGISTIC Procedure

Analysis of Maximum Likelihood Estimates

Variable	DF	Parameter Estimate	Standard Error	Wald Chi-Square	Pr > ChiSq	Standardized Estimate	Odds Ratio	Label
Intercept	1	12.8762	7.4039	3.0245	0.0820			Intercept
CONTROL	1	1.9706	2.1771	0.8193	0.3654	1.3740	7.175	CONTROL
ATTMAR	1	0.2215	0.2344	0.8923	0.3449	1.0410	1.248	ATTMAR
ATTROLE	1	-1.5562	0.6231	6.2375	0.0125	-5.7752	0.211	ATTROLE
ATTHOUSE	1	-0.8193	0.6314	1.6836	0.1944	-2.0240	0.441	ATTHOUSE
LIN_CTRL	1	-0.6863	0.7396	0.8610	0.3534	-1.4084	0.503	
LIN_ATMR	1	-0.0475	0.0549	0.7481	0.3871	-0.9515	0.954	
LIN_ATRL	1	0.3263	0.1362	5.7391	0.0166	5.5068	1.386	
LIN_ATHS	1	0.1905	0.1529	1.5531	0.2127	1.9193	1.210	

Output differs only slightly from that of Table 12.14 in *UMS*.

The main logistic regression analysis is now performed without the interactions. From the

SAS/ASSIST: WorkPlace window, choosing

> **Data Analysis**

157

> **Regression**
> **Logistic...**

produces the **Logistic Regression** dialog box of Figure 12.4. After selecting LOGREG as the **Table:**, and clicking on ⊙**One column** for **Response form is:**, WORKSTAT is selected as the **Response:** variable. **Independent:** variables chosen are CONTROL, ATTMAR, ATTHOUSE, and ATTROLE. (Note that either the LOGREG or LOGREGIN file may be used here.)

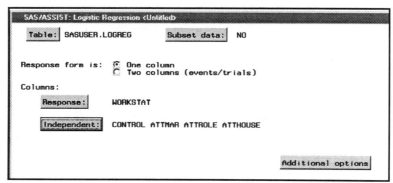

Figure 12.4   **SAS/ASSIST: Logistic Regression** dialog box.

Clicking on **Additional options:** produces the **Additional Options** menu of Figure 12.5, where clicking on **Printed output...** produces the **Logistic Output** dialog box of Figure 12.6.

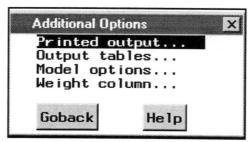

Figure 12.5   **Additional Options** menu
                for logistic regression.

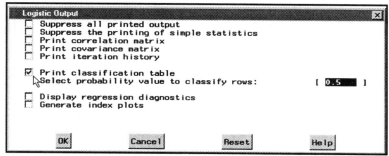

Figure 12.6   **Logistic Output** dialog box.

☑**Print classification table** is requested, with the default probability of 0.5 left intact. Clicking on **OK** returns the **Additional Options** menu, where clicking on **Goback** returns the **Logistic Regression** dialog box. Clicking on runner icon produces *Output 12.2.*

Output 12.2   LOGISTIC REGRESSION ANALYSIS OF WORK STATUS WITH ADDITUDINAL VARIABLES.

The LOGISTIC Procedure

Model Information

Data Set	SASUSER.LOGREG	
Response Variable	WORKSTAT	WORKSTAT
Number of Response Levels	2	
Number of Observations	462	
Link Function	Logit	
Optimization Technique	Fisher's scoring	

Response Profile

Ordered Value	WORKSTAT	Total Frequency
1	0	245
2	1	217

Model Fit Statistics

Criterion	Intercept Only	Intercept and Covariates
AIC	640.770	625.534
SC	644.906	646.212
-2 Log L	638.770	615.534

159

Testing Global Null Hypothesis: BETA=0

Test	Chi-Square	DF	Pr > ChiSq
Likelihood Ratio	23.2362	4	0.0001
Score	22.7391	4	0.0001
Wald	21.7498	4	0.0002

The LOGISTIC Procedure

Analysis of Maximum Likelihood Estimates

Variable	DF	Parameter Estimate	Standard Error	Wald Chi-Square	Pr > ChiSq	Standardized Estimate	Odds Ratio	Label
Intercept	1	3.1964	0.9580	11.1319	0.0008			Intercept
CONTROL	1	-0.0574	0.0781	0.5410	0.4620	-0.0400	0.944	CONTROL
ATTMAR	1	0.0162	0.0120	1.8191	0.1774	0.0763	1.016	ATTMAR
ATTROLE	1	-0.0681	0.0155	19.2977	<.0001	-0.2526	0.934	ATTROLE
ATTHOUSE	1	-0.0282	0.0238	1.4002	0.2367	-0.0697	0.972	ATTHOUSE

Association of Predicted Probabilities and Observed Responses

Percent Concordant	62.9	Somers' D	0.263
Percent Discordant	36.6	Gamma	0.265
Percent Tied	0.5	Tau-a	0.131
Pairs	53165	c	0.632

Classification Table

	Correct		Incorrect			Percentages			
Prob		Non-		Non-		Sensi-	Speci-	False	False
Level	Event	Event	Event	Event	Correct	tivity	ficity	POS	NEG
0.200	245	0	217	0	53.0	100.0	0.0	47.0	.
0.220	244	0	217	1	52.8	99.6	0.0	47.1	100.0
0.240	244	0	217	1	52.8	99.6	0.0	47.1	100.0
0.260	244	2	215	1	53.2	99.6	0.9	46.8	33.3
0.280	243	3	214	2	53.2	99.2	1.4	46.8	40.0
0.300	241	5	212	4	53.2	98.4	2.3	46.8	44.4
0.320	237	9	208	8	53.2	96.7	4.1	46.7	47.1
0.340	232	10	207	13	52.4	94.7	4.6	47.2	56.5
0.360	231	15	202	14	53.2	94.3	6.9	46.7	48.3
0.380	226	25	192	19	54.3	92.2	11.5	45.9	43.2
0.400	220	34	183	25	55.0	89.8	15.7	45.4	42.4
0.420	207	48	169	38	55.2	84.5	22.1	44.9	44.2
0.440	197	67	150	48	57.1	80.4	30.9	43.2	41.7
0.460	189	74	143	56	56.9	77.1	34.1	43.1	43.1
0.480	180	90	127	65	58.4	73.5	41.5	41.4	41.9
0.500	164	103	114	81	57.8	66.9	47.5	41.0	44.0
0.520	151	117	100	94	58.0	61.6	53.9	39.8	44.5

0.540	142	129	88	103	58.7	58.0	59.4	38.3	44.4
0.560	127	138	79	118	57.4	51.8	63.6	38.3	46.1
0.580	114	153	64	131	57.8	46.5	70.5	36.0	46.1
0.600	90	164	53	155	55.0	36.7	75.6	37.1	48.6
0.620	71	185	32	174	55.4	29.0	85.3	31.1	48.5
0.640	53	196	21	192	53.9	21.6	90.3	28.4	49.5
0.660	39	201	16	206	51.9	15.9	92.6	29.1	50.6
0.680	28	208	9	217	51.1	11.4	95.9	24.3	51.1
0.700	16	214	3	229	49.8	6.5	98.6	15.8	51.7
0.720	9	215	2	236	48.5	3.7	99.1	18.2	52.3
0.740	7	216	1	238	48.3	2.9	99.5	12.5	52.4
0.760	2	216	1	243	47.2	0.8	99.5	33.3	52.9
0.780	1	216	1	244	47.0	0.4	99.5	50.0	53.0
0.800	1	216	1	244	47.0	0.4	99.5	50.0	53.0
0.820	0	216	1	245	46.8	0.0	99.5	100.0	53.1
0.840	0	217	0	245	47.0	0.0	100.0	.	53.0

`Parameter Estimates` differ only slightly from those in Table 12.14 of *UMS*. The working group is labeled `Event` in the `Classification Table`, which provides information for a variety of criterion probability levels, not just the requested 0.5. Note that the classification results for a criterion probability level of 0.5 differ considerably from the prediction success table in Table 12.14 of *UMS*. The SAS classification is more successful (less conservative) for both groups, even though SAS LOGISTIC uses jackknifed classification.

An analysis that excludes ATTROLE simply omits that variable from the list of **Independent:** variables in the **Logistic Regression** dialog box, as per Figure 12.7.

Figure 12.7   **Logistic Regression** dialog box with ATTROLE omitted.

Unneeded output may be suppressed by removing the request for **Print classification table** in the **Logistic Output** dialog box of Figure 12.6. Clicking on the runner icon on the toolbar produces *Output 12.3*, which produces a log-likelihood ratio to compare models with and without ATTROLE.

Output 12.3	LOGISTIC REGRESSION ANALYSIS FOR MODEL THAT EXCLUDES ATTROLE (PARTIAL OUTPUT).

The LOGISTIC Procedure

Model Fit Statistics

Criterion	Intercept Only	Intercept and Covariates
AIC	640.770	644.002
SC	644.906	660.544
-2 Log L	638.770	636.002

The value shown in SAS output is not log-likelihood per se, but -2 log likelihood. Therefore, application of Equation 12.7 from *Using Multivariate Statistics* is modified to:

$$\chi^2 = [(-2 \text{ Log Likelihood of smaller model}) - (-2 \text{ Log Likelihood of bigger model})]$$

Applied to values from *Output 12.2* and *12.3*, this produces the same difference value as shown in Section 12.7.2 of *UMS*.

$$\chi^2 = 636.002 - 615.534 = 20.468$$

12.3 SEQUENTIAL LOGISTIC REGRESSION WITH THREE CATEGORIES OF OUTCOME

The parameter estimates of Section 12.7.3 in *UMS* are found in SAS by two separate analyses of WORKSTAT, one in which WORKING is contrasted with UNHOUSE, and a second in which HAPHOUSE is contrasted with UNHOUSE. (Another set contrasts might be of interest, but these mimic the analysis in Section 12.7.3.) Of course, these analyses give no overall statistics regarding the three groups evaluated simultaneously.

The first requirement for both analyses (plus the tests of linearity of the logit) is to dummy code the predictors that have more than two categories, because SAS LOGISTIC assumes that all predictors are continuous. Figure 12.8 shows the syntax for creating a new data set, SASUSER.LOGREGM, from the LOGREGCC data set, which contains five variables to replace MARITAL with three categories and RELIGION with four categories: MAR1, MAR2, RELIG1, RELIG2, RELIG3.

```
data SASUSER.LOGREGM;
  set SASUSER.LOGREGCC;
    MAR1 = 0;
    MAR2 = 0;
    if MARITAL = 1 then MAR1 = 1;
    if MARITAL = 2 then MAR2 = 1;
    RELIG1 = 0;
    RELIG2 = 0;
    RELIG3 = 0;
    if RELIGION = 1 then RELIG1 = 1;
    if RELIGION = 2 then RELIG2 = 1;
    if RELIGION = 3 then RELIG3 = 1;
run;
```

Figure 12.8   Batch file to create data set with dummy coded predictors.

Then, two more data sets are created: one with WORKING coded 0 and UNHOUSE coded 1 (SASUSER.LOGREGMM), and the second with HAPHOUSE coded 0 and UNHOUSE coded 1. Only the syntax for the first of these is shown in Figure 12.9.

```
data SASUSER.LOGREGMM;
  set SASUSER.LOGREGM;
  if WORKSTAT = 2 then delete;
  if WORKSTAT = 1 then WORKSTAT = 0;
  if WORKSTAT = 3 then WORKSTAT = 1;
run;
```

Figure 12.9   Batch file to recode
               WORKSTAT for analysis of
               WORKING vs. UNHOUSE.

Two more data sets are necessary to test linearity of the logit. For each of the newly created files (e.g., LOGREGMM), the interactions between continuous variables and their interactions with their natural logarithms are created, as per the batch file of Figure 12.10. The new data set is labeled LOGREGMI.

```
data SASUSER.LOGREGMI;
  set SASUSER.LOGREGMM;
  LIN_CTRL=LOG(CONTROL)*CONTROL;
  LIN_ATMR=LOG(ATTMAR)*ATTMAR;
  LIN_ATRL=LOG(ATTROLE)*ATTROLE;
  LIN_ATHS=LOG(ATTHOUSE)*ATTHOUSE;
  LIN_SEL=LOG(SEL+1)*SEL;
  LIN_AGE=LOG(AGE+1)*AGE;
  LIN_EDUC=LOG(EDUC)*EDUC;
run;
```

Figure 12.10   Batch file to create
               interactions to test linearity in
               the logit.

Linearity in the logit is tested by adding these variables to the existing demographic and attitudinal variables, as per Section 12.2 of this workbook. Figure 12.11 shows the **SAS/ASSIST: Logistic Regression** dialog box, with SASUSER.LOGREGMM (or LOGREGMI) as the **Table:** and WORKSTAT as the **Response:** variable. **Independent:** variables chosen are CHILDREN, RACE, CONTROL, ATTMAR, ATTROLE, SEL, ATTHOUSE, AGE, EDUC, MAR1, MAR2, RELIG1, RELIG2,

164

RELIG3, LIN_CTRL, LIN_ATMR, LIN_ATTRL, LIN_SEL, LIN_ATHS, LIN_AGE, LIN_EDUC. (Not all of these show up in Figure 12.11.) Results are in *Output 12.4*.

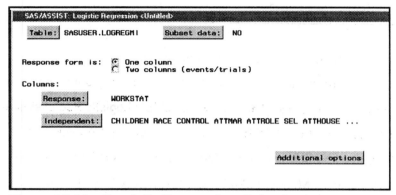

Figure 12.11 **Logistic Regression** dialog box to test linearity in the logit for sequential analysis.

Output 12.4 LOGISTIC REGRESSION ANALYSIS TO TEST LINEARITY OF THE LOGIT FOR SEQUENTIAL ANALYSIS.

The LOGISTIC Procedure

Analysis of Maximum Likelihood Estimates

Variable	DF	Parameter Estimate	Standard Error	Wald Chi-Square	Pr > ChiSq	Standardized Estimate	Odds Ratio	Label
Intercept	1	24.5676	13.5415	3.2915	0.0696			Intercept
CHILDREN	1	-0.6155	0.5073	1.4721	0.2250	-0.1387	0.540	CHILDREN
RACE	1	0.6495	0.5171	1.5776	0.2091	0.1123	1.915	RACE
CONTROL	1	-2.1315	3.3372	0.4080	0.5230	-1.4651	0.119	CONTROL
ATTMAR	1	0.4699	0.3094	2.3065	0.1288	2.3350	1.600	ATTMAR
ATTROLE	1	-2.2535	1.0008	5.0707	0.0243	-8.3468	0.105	ATTROLE
SEL	1	0.0922	0.1102	0.6992	0.4031	1.1575	1.097	SEL
ATTHOUSE	1	-0.4828	1.2069	0.1600	0.6891	-1.2397	0.617	ATTHOUSE
AGE	1	0.9928	0.6996	2.0139	0.1559	1.2117	2.699	AGE
EDUC	1	-0.1840	1.4577	0.0159	0.8995	-0.2415	0.832	EDUC
MAR1	1	0.3212	0.7933	0.1639	0.6856	0.0496	1.379	
MAR2	1	-0.4748	0.4207	1.2738	0.2590	-0.1190	0.622	
RELIG1	1	0.3121	0.5269	0.3507	0.5537	0.0645	1.366	
RELIG2	1	-0.1733	0.4367	0.1575	0.6915	-0.0427	0.841	
RELIG3	1	-0.0521	0.4099	0.0161	0.8989	-0.0139	0.949	
LIN_CTRL	1	0.6951	1.1277	0.3799	0.5376	1.4073	2.004	

LIN_ATMR	1	-0.1152	0.0718	2.5732	0.1087	-2.4541	0.891
LIN_ATRL	1	0.4828	0.2191	4.8572	0.0275	8.0939	1.621
LIN_ATHS	1	0.0926	0.2890	0.1026	0.7487	0.9669	1.097
LIN_SEL	1	-0.0202	0.0232	0.7621	0.3827	-1.2135	0.980
LIN_AGE	1	-0.3406	0.2821	1.4579	0.2273	-1.0109	0.711
LIN_EDUC	1	0.0906	0.4084	0.0493	0.8243	0.4327	1.095

Note that LIN_SEL is not statistically reliable in this comparison.

The main analysis of all variables, attitudinal as well as demographic, proceeds as per Figure 12.11, omitting the interaction variables. Thus, the **SAS/ASSIST: Logistic Regression** dialog box is filled out with SASUSER.LOGREGMM (or LOGREGMI) as the **Table:** and WORKSTAT as the **Response:** variable. **Independent:** variables chosen are CHILDREN, RACE, CONTROL, ATTMAR, ATTROLE, SEL, ATTHOUSE, AGE, EDUC, MAR1, MAR2, RELIG1, RELIG2, RELIG3.

Clicking on **Additional options** lets you request printing of a classification table as per Figures 12.5 and 12.6, however this table is restricted to the two groups analyzed. Clicking on the runner icon from the **SAS/ASSIST: Logistic Regression** dialog box produces *Output 12.5*.

Output 12.5 LOGISTIC REGRESSION ANALYSIS OF WORKING WOMEN VS. ROLE-DISSATISFIED HOUSEWIVES WITH DEMOGRAPHIC AND ATTITUDINAL VARIABLES, SELECTED OUTPUT.

The LOGISTIC Procedure

Model Information

Data Set	SASUSER.LOGREGMM	
Response Variable	WORKSTAT	WORKSTAT
Number of Response Levels	2	
Number of Observations	327	
Link Function	Logit	
Optimization Technique	Fisher's scoring	

Response Profile

Ordered Value	WORKSTAT	Total Frequency
1	0	245
2	1	82

166

Model Fit Statistics

Criterion	Intercept Only	Intercept and Covariates
AIC	370.315	364.186
SC	374.105	421.036
-2 Log L	368.315	334.186

Testing Global Null Hypothesis: BETA=0

Test	Chi-Square	DF	Pr > ChiSq
Likelihood Ratio	34.1292	14	0.0020
Score	31.9384	14	0.0041
Wald	28.4627	14	0.0123

The LOGISTIC Procedure

Analysis of Maximum Likelihood Estimates

Variable	DF	Parameter Estimate	Standard Error	Wald Chi-Square	Pr > ChiSq	Standardized Estimate	Odds Ratio	Label
Intercept	1	3.6836	2.0617	3.1924	0.0740			Intercept
CHILDREN	1	-0.4340	0.4612	0.8852	0.3468	-0.0978	0.648	CHILDREN
RACE	1	0.6188	0.4812	1.6536	0.1985	0.1070	1.857	RACE
CONTROL	1	-0.0938	0.1119	0.7037	0.4015	-0.0645	0.910	CONTROL
ATTMAR	1	-0.0274	0.0175	2.4565	0.1170	-0.1361	0.973	ATTMAR
ATTROLE	1	-0.0504	0.0247	4.1566	0.0415	-0.1865	0.951	ATTROLE
SEL	1	-0.00319	0.00654	0.2380	0.6257	-0.0401	0.997	SEL
ATTHOUSE	1	-0.0766	0.0358	4.5885	0.0322	-0.1967	0.926	ATTHOUSE
AGE	1	0.1412	0.0743	3.6093	0.0575	0.1723	1.152	AGE
EDUC	1	0.1498	0.0760	3.8859	0.0487	0.1967	1.162	EDUC
MAR1	1	0.1163	0.7489	0.0241	0.8766	0.0180	1.123	
MAR2	1	-0.5012	0.4030	1.5466	0.2136	-0.1256	0.606	
RELIG1	1	0.3408	0.5085	0.4492	0.5027	0.0704	1.406	
RELIG2	1	-0.1888	0.4252	0.1972	0.6570	-0.0466	0.828	
RELIG3	1	-0.0576	0.4004	0.0207	0.8857	-0.0154	0.944	

Association of Predicted Probabilities and Observed Responses

Percent Concordant	69.7	Somers' D	0.399
Percent Discordant	29.9	Gamma	0.400
Percent Tied	0.4	Tau-a	0.150
Pairs	20090	c	0.699

167

The `Parameter Estimates` are similar to those of the top half of the table labeled `Parameter Estimates` in Table 12.18 of *UMS*. For example, compare the intercept values of 3.6836 of SAS vs. 4.434 of SPSS. The remaining statistics bear no resemblance to those of SPSS because only two of the WORKSTAT categories are analyzed.

Some of the remaining output is useful for comparing models with and without attitudinal variables, however. First, a new model is run with demographic variables alone, still comparing WORKING vs. UNHOUSE groups. The demographic variables are removed from the list of **Independent:** variables, producing Figure 12.12 and *Output 12.6*.

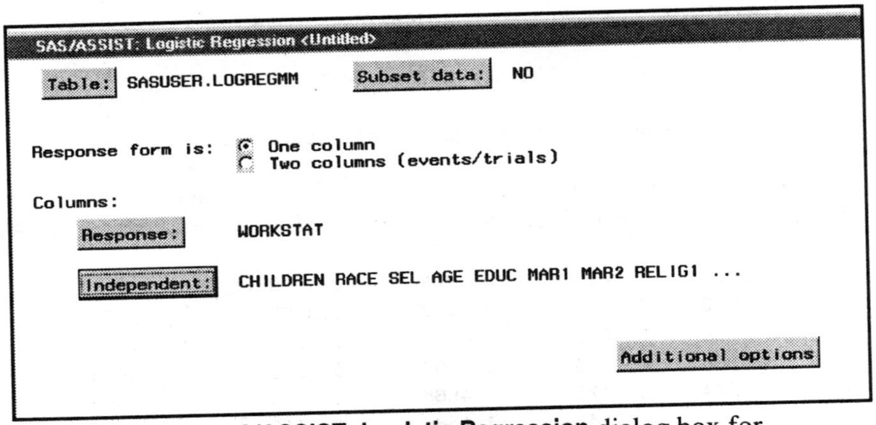

Figure 12.12   **SAS/ASSIST: Logistic Regression** dialog box for demographic variables.

Output 12.6   LOGISTIC REGRESSION ANALYSIS OF DEMOGRAPHIC VARIABLES ONLY FOR WORKING WOMEN VS. ROLE-DISSATISFIED HOUSEWIVES. PARTIAL OUTPUT.

The LOGISTIC Procedure

Model Information

Data Set	SASUSER.LOGREGMM	
Response Variable	WORKSTAT	WORKSTAT
Number of Response Levels	2	
Number of Observations	327	
Link Function	Logit	
Optimization Technique	Fisher's scoring	

```
                    Response Profile

    Ordered                              Total
     Value            WORKSTAT         Frequency

        1                 0               245
        2                 1                82


                 Model Fit Statistics

                                        Intercept
                          Intercept        and
     Criterion              Only        Covariates

       AIC                 370.315        370.247
       SC                  374.105        411.936
       -2 Log L            368.315        348.247


         Testing Global Null Hypothesis: BETA=0

    Test              Chi-Square      DF     Pr > ChiSq

    Likelihood Ratio     20.0687      10       0.0286
    Score                18.3612      10       0.0492
    Wald                 17.1826      10       0.0704
```

The models with and without attitudinal variables are compared using Equation 12.7 with `Likelihood Ratio`s:

$$\chi^2 = 34.1292 - 20.0687 = 14.06$$

With 14 - 10 = 4 df, $p < .05$. (The same value results when the values used are `-2 Log L`.) Thus, the attitudinal variables significantly add to prediction of whether a woman is employed outside the home for at least 20 hours per week or is a role-dissatisfied housewife.

The same procedure is followed for analysis of differences between role-satisfied and role-dissatisfied housewives. Another data set is created in which HAPHOUSE are coded 0 and UNHOUSE are coded 1, as seen in Figure 12.10.

```
data SASUSER.LOGREGM2;
  set SASUSER.LOGREGM;
  if WORKSTAT = 1 then delete;
  if WORKSTAT = 2 then WORKSTAT = 0;
  if WORKSTAT = 3 then WORKSTAT = 1;
run;
```

Figure 12.10   Batch file for creating data
set comparing HAPHOUSE
vs. UNHOUSE.

The procedures illustrated above in Figures 12.11 and 12.12 are then followed with **Table:** selected as SASUSER.LOGREGM2 in the **SAS/ASSIST: Logistic Regression** dialog box. The resulting χ^2 for the difference between models, if statistically reliable, is interpreted as the gain in distinguishing between role-satisfied and role-dissatisfied housewives by adding attitudinal variables.

Chapter 13. Principal Components and Factor Analysis

This chapter demonstrates factor analysis using SAS for Windows for the complete example of Chapter 13, *Using Multivariate Statistics*. The file to use is FACTOR.SAS7BDAT. This example demonstrates a factor analysis of the Bem Sex Role Inventory.

13.1 EVALUATION OF ASSUMPTIONS

Distributions of the 44 variables are examined for skewness through the **Interactive Data Analysis** procedure of Section 4.1.1. Spot checks for linearity are made through scatterplots, as demonstrated in Section 4.1.4. Outliers among cases may be found through regression using SUBNO as the dummy DV, as per Section 4.1.6. This creates the new variable, **H**, which is the leverage value for each case. This is converted to Mahalanobis distance using Equation 4.3, as shown at the end of Section 4.1.6. The most convenient way in SAS to discriminate between outliers and non-outlying cases when there are many outliers is through stepwise discriminant function analysis, as shown in Table 13.12 of *UMS*. This procedure is unavailable in SAS ASSIST.

Principal components analysis is performed from the **SAS/ASSIST: WorkPlace** by choosing

> **> Data Analysis**
> **> Multivariate**
> **> Principal Components...**

However, the maximum number of variables that may be analyzed through SAS/ASSIST is 26. Therefore, the remaining analysis are done through batch processing. Even in batch processing, SAS PRINCOMP procedure does not provide SMCs for evaluating multicollinearity and outliers among variables, nor does it provide measures of factorability of the correlation matrix. SAS FACTOR (which does a principal components analysis by default) will therefore be used for remaining preliminary evaluation.

13.2 FACTOR ANALYSIS AND FACTOR SCORE PLOTS

The final analyses also are done through SAS FACTOR, thus are those shown in Section 13.7.2 of *UMS*.

Interactive Data Analysis may be used to create the entire set of factor score plots, as an alternative to the single plot in Figure 13.5 of *UMS*, once factor scores are saved as per Table 13.17 of *UMS*.

To create the factor score plots, from the main SAS toolbar choose

> **S**olutions
　　> **Analy**s**is**
　　　　> **I**nteractive Data Analysis

This produces the **SAS/INSIGHT: Open** menu of Figure 3.12 to select the FACSCORE data set. Clicking on **OK** produces the **SASUSER.FACSCORE** screen. Figure 13.1 displays factor scores for the first 14 cases from that screen.

► 49	Int	Int	Int	Int
344	FACTOR1	FACTOR2	FACTOR3	FACTOR4
■ 1	0.24393	0.7729	1.5338	0.7069
■ 2	-1.06394	-1.2265	-1.0208	-0.6392
■ 3	-1.09748	-0.2006	-0.0379	0.9851
■ 4	-0.60254	-0.0732	0.0406	0.5870
■ 5	1.72427	0.8547	0.4499	-0.8634
■ 6	-1.19654	-0.2175	0.1135	1.5622
■ 7	-1.88986	0.4119	-0.6607	-1.4629
■ 8	0.57471	0.3907	0.0859	0.4285
■ 9	0.92663	-0.2062	-1.8942	-0.4038
■ 10	0.15632	0.0042	0.8837	-1.5429
■ 11	-0.42125	1.4809	-0.5228	-0.3278
■ 12	-1.24868	1.5763	0.0787	-3.2521
■ 13	1.79677	0.8951	1.3263	0.5962
■ 14	0.38291	-0.0236	-0.9491	-1.1727

Figure 13.1　　Factor scores for first 14 cases.

Clicking on

> **A**nalyze
　　> **S**catter Plot (Y X)

produces the **Scatter Plot (Y X)** dialog box of Figure 13.2.

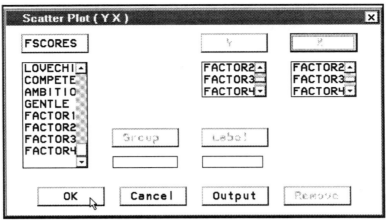

Figure 13.2   **Scatter Plot (Y X)** dialog box for factor score
plots.

All four factor score variables (FACTOR1 through FACTOR4) are chosen as **Y** and **X** variables.
This ensures that all combinations of factor scores are plotted, along with a few duplicate plots which
may be ignored. Clicking on **OK** produces the scatterplot matrix of Figure 13.3.

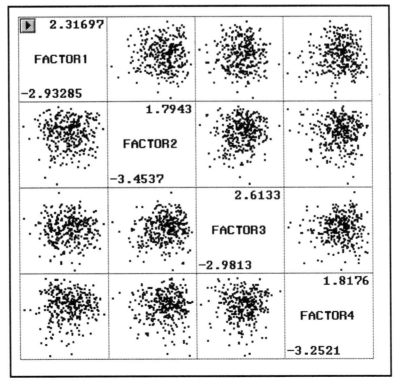

Figure 13.3   Scatterplots of factor scores.

173

Chapter 14. Structural Equation Modeling

This chapter demonstrates structural equation modeling using SAS for Windows for the complete examples of Chapter 14 in *UMS*. The files to use are WISCSEM.SAS7BDAT and HLTHSEM.SAS7BDAT.

The first example demonstrates confirmatory factor analysis of 11 subtests of the Wechsler Intelligence Scale for Children (WISC) in a sample of learning-disabled children. The second example examines the mediators of the relationship between age, a life change measure, and latent variables representing Poor Sense of Self, Perceived Ill Health, and Health Care Utilization.

SAS does not provide structural equation modeling through the graphical interface. Therefore, the analysis are done through SAS CALIS with batch instruction files.

14.1   EVALUATION OF ASSUMPTIONS

Distributions of the 11 variables are examined for normality through the **Interactive Data Analysis** procedure (cf. Section 4.1.1). SAS CALIS also provides information on multivariate normality in the main analysis, labeled Mardia's Multivariate Kurtosis (see *Output 14.1*).

Spot checks for linearity are made through scatterplots, as demonstrated in Section 4.1.4. Outliers among cases may be found through regression using subject number as the dummy DV, as per Section 4.1.6. This creates the new variable, H, which is the leverage value for each case. This is converted to Mahalanobis distance using Equation 4.3, as shown at the end of Section 4.1.6. The procedure for creating a new file with the outliers deleted is described in Section 13.1 (note that outliers have been deleted in the HLTHSEM data set.) The convergence criterion is satisfied in the main analyses, indicating absence of multicollinearity in both data sets.

14.2   CONFIRMATORY FACTOR ANALYSIS OF THE WISC

Model specification is as described in Section 14.6.1 in *UMS*

14.2.1 Model Estimation and Preliminary Evaluation

Figure 14.1 shows the batch file of instructions for performing confirmatory factor analysis on the WISC through SAS CALIS, using the LINEQS convention. The labels for the factors are F1 for Verbal Scale IQ and F2 for Performance Scale IQ.

175

```
proc calis data=SASUSER.WISCSEM cov all;
   lineqs
      INFO              = X1 F1+E1,
      COMP              = X2 F1+E2,
      ARITH             = X3 F1+E3,
      SIMIL             = X4 F1+E4,
      VOCAB             = X5 F1+E5,
      DIGIT             = X6 F1+E6,
      PICTCOMP          = X7 F2+E7,
      PARANG            = X8 F2+E8,
      BLOCK             = X9 F2+E9,
      OBJECT            =X10 F2+E10,
      CODING            =X11 F2+E11;
   std
      E1-E11 = X12-X22,
      F1=1,
      F2=1;
   cov
      F1 F2=phi1;
run;
```

Figure 14.1   Batch file for confirmatory factor analysis.

Clicking on the runner icon on the toolbar produces *Output 14.1*.

___

Output 14.1   CONFIRMATORY FACTOR ANALYSIS THROUGH SAS CALIS (SELECTED OUTPUT).
___

The CALIS Procedure
Covariance Structure Analysis: Pattern and Initial Values

Automatic Variable Selection, the Following Manifest Variables are not Used in the Model

CLIENT   AGEMATE

Using the VAR statement for variable selection could save memory and computing time.

LINEQS Model Statement

		Matrix	Rows	Columns	------Matrix Type-------	
Term 1	1	_SEL_	11	24	SELECTION	
	2	_BETA_	24	24	EQSBETA	IMINUSINV
	3	_GAMMA_	24	13	EQSGAMMA	
	4	_PHI_	13	13	SYMMETRIC	

The 11 Endogenous Variables

Manifest	INFO	COMP	ARITH	SIMIL	VOCAB
	DIGIT	PICTCOMP	PARANG		
	BLOCK	OBJECT	CODING		

176

Latent

The 13 Exogenous Variables

Manifest						
Latent	F1	F2				
Error	E1	E2	E3	E4	E5	E6
	E7	E8	E9	E10	E11	

Covariance Structure Analysis: Pattern and Initial Values

Manifest Variable Equations

Initial Estimates

$$INFO = .*F1 + 1.0000 \ E1$$
$$X1$$

$$COMP = .*F1 + 1.0000 \ E2$$
$$X2$$

$$ARITH = .*F1 + 1.0000 \ E3$$
$$X3$$

$$SIMIL = .*F1 + 1.0000 \ E4$$
$$X4$$

$$VOCAB = .*F1 + 1.0000 \ E5$$
$$X5$$

$$DIGIT = .*F1 + 1.0000 \ E6$$
$$X6$$

$$PICTCOMP = .*F2 + 1.0000 \ E7$$
$$X7$$

$$PARANG = .*F2 + 1.0000 \ E8$$
$$X8$$

$$BLOCK = .*F2 + 1.0000 \ E9$$
$$X9$$

$$OBJECT = .*F2 + 1.0000 \ E10$$
$$X10$$

$$CODING = .*F2 + 1.0000 \ E11$$
$$X11$$

Variances of Exogenous Variables

Variable	Parameter	Estimate
F1		1.00000
F2		1.00000
E1	X12	.
E2	X13	.
E3	X14	.
E4	X15	.
E5	X16	.
E6	X17	.
E7	X18	.

177

```
              E8        X19               .
              E9        X20               .
              E10       X21               .
              E11       X22               .
```

Covariances Among Exogenous Variables

```
         Var1      Var2      Parameter      Estimate

          F1        F2        phi1              .
```

```
          Observations      175   Model Terms           1
          Variables          11   Model Matrices        4
          Informations       66   Parameters           23
```

		Mean	Std Dev	Skewness	Kurtosis
INFO	Information	9.49714286	2.912269498	0.0848559945	-.0141461456
COMP	Comprehension	10.00000000	2.965316753	0.0869548941	0.4102584656
ARITH	Arithmetic	9.00000000	2.306911156	0.3977675732	-.1156374395
SIMIL	Similarities	10.61142857	3.183630133	0.0227180010	-.1686029164
VOCAB	Vocabulary	10.70285714	2.932721238	0.2716551516	0.3699874180
DIGIT	Digit span	8.73142857	2.704165734	0.2709365605	0.1456805150
PICTCOMP	Picture completion	10.68000000	2.934221391	-.0727445810	0.3737786530
PARANG	Picture arrangement	10.37142857	2.659678858	-.2025460294	0.0097768620
BLOCK	Block design	10.31428571	2.709831277	-.2235392754	0.5932318677
OBJECT	Object Assembly	10.90285714	2.843977880	-.1250271128	0.2241732314
CODING	Coding	8.54857143	2.872118389	-.0537486304	-.4017078716

```
          Mardia's Multivariate Kurtosis                   5.9008
          Relative Multivariate Kurtosis                   1.0413
          Normalized Multivariate Kurtosis                 2.3079
          Mardia Based Kappa (Browne, 1982)                0.0413
          Mean Scaled Univariate Kurtosis                  0.0432
          Adjusted Mean Scaled Univariate Kurtosis         0.0432
```

Observation Numbers with Largest Contribution to Kurtosis

```
          76            66           73           101           36

      249.9141      240.1692     189.2218      184.5557     168.7521
```

Covariances

		INFO	COMP	ARITH	SIMIL
INFO	Information	8.481313629	4.034482759	3.321839080	4.75750411
COMP	Comprehension	4.034482759	8.793103448	2.683908046	4.81609195
ARITH	Arithmetic	3.321839080	2.683908046	5.321839080	2.71264368
SIMIL	Similarities	4.757504105	4.816091954	2.712643678	10.13550082
VOCAB	Vocabulary	5.338226601	4.620689655	2.620689655	5.02180624
DIGIT	Digit span	2.720492611	1.890804598	1.678160920	2.23412151
PICTCOMP	Picture completion	1.964597701	3.540229885	1.051724138	3.44965517
PARANG	Picture arrangement	1.561412151	1.471264368	1.390804598	2.52446634
BLOCK	Block design	1.808374384	2.965517241	1.701149425	2.25500821

178

| OBJECT | Object Assembly | 1.531330049 | 2.718390805 | 0.281609195 | 2.43330049 |
| CODING | Coding | 0.059047619 | 0.517241379 | 0.597701149 | -0.37182266 |

Covariances

		VOCAB	DIGIT	PICTCOMP	PARANG
INFO	Information	5.338226601	2.720492611	1.964597701	1.561412151
COMP	Comprehension	4.620689655	1.890804598	3.540229885	1.471264368
ARITH	Arithmetic	2.620689655	1.678160920	1.051724138	1.390804598
SIMIL	Similarities	5.021806240	2.234121511	3.449655172	2.524466338
VOCAB	Vocabulary	8.600853859	2.333530378	2.456091954	1.030541872
DIGIT	Digit span	2.333530378	7.312512315	0.597471264	1.065845649
PICTCOMP	Picture completion	2.456091954	0.597471264	8.609655172	1.941379310
PARANG	Picture arrangement	1.030541872	1.065845649	1.941379310	7.073891626
BLOCK	Block design	2.364039409	0.533169130	3.037931034	2.532019704
OBJECT	Object Assembly	1.545681445	0.266863711	3.031954023	1.915599343
CODING	Coding	0.842101806	1.343579639	-0.605057471	0.289326765

Covariances

		BLOCK	OBJECT	CODING
INFO	Information	1.808374384	1.531330049	0.059047619
COMP	Comprehension	2.965517241	2.718390805	0.517241379
ARITH	Arithmetic	1.701149425	0.281609195	0.597701149
SIMIL	Similarities	2.255008210	2.433300493	-0.371822660
VOCAB	Vocabulary	2.364039409	1.545681445	0.842101806
DIGIT	Digit span	0.533169130	0.266863711	1.343579639
PICTCOMP	Picture completion	3.037931034	3.031954023	-0.605057471
PARANG	Picture arrangement	2.532019704	1.915599343	0.289326765
BLOCK	Block design	7.343185550	3.076683087	0.832348112
OBJECT	Object Assembly	3.076683087	8.088210181	0.432906404
CODING	Coding	0.832348112	0.432906404	8.249064039

Determinant 388513953 Ln 19.777840

Some initial estimates computed by instrumental variable method.

Fit Function	0.4037
Goodness of Fit Index (GFI)	0.9309
GFI Adjusted for Degrees of Freedom (AGFI)	0.8939
Root Mean Square Residual (RMR)	0.4683
Parsimonious GFI (Mulaik, 1989)	0.7278
Chi-Square	70.2359
Chi-Square DF	43
Pr > Chi-Square	0.0054
Independence Model Chi-Square	516.24
Independence Model Chi-Square DF	55
RMSEA Estimate	0.0603
RMSEA 90% Lower Confidence Limit	0.0330
RMSEA 90% Upper Confidence Limit	0.0851
ECVI Estimate	0.6876
ECVI 90% Lower Confidence Limit	0.5770
ECVI 90% Upper Confidence Limit	0.8472

Probability of Close Fit	0.2391
Bentler's Comparative Fit Index	0.9410
Elliptic Corrected Chi-Square	67.4525
Pr > Elliptic Corrected Chi-Square	0.0100
Normal Theory Reweighted LS Chi-Square	71.0450
Akaike's Information Criterion	-15.7641
Bozdogan's (1987) CAIC	-194.8499
Schwarz's Bayesian Criterion	-151.8499
McDonald's (1989) Centrality	0.9251
Bentler & Bonett's (1980) Non-normed Index	0.9245
Bentler & Bonett's (1980) NFI	0.8639
James, Mulaik, & Brett (1982) Parsimonious NFI	0.6754
Z-Test of Wilson & Hilferty (1931)	2.5436
Bollen (1986) Normed Index Rho1	0.8260
Bollen (1988) Non-normed Index Delta2	0.9424
Hoelter's (1983) Critical N	148

Distribution of Asymptotically Standardized Residuals

Each * Represents 1 Residuals

----------Range---------		Freq	Percent	
-2.50000	-2.25000	2	3.03	**
-2.25000	-2.00000	1	1.52	*
-2.00000	-1.75000	0	0.00	
-1.75000	-1.50000	2	3.03	**
-1.50000	-1.25000	5	7.58	*****
-1.25000	-1.00000	2	3.03	**
-1.00000	-0.75000	4	6.06	****
-0.75000	-0.50000	3	4.55	***
-0.50000	-0.25000	5	7.58	*****
-0.25000	0	5	7.58	*****
0	0.25000	14	21.21	**************
0.25000	0.50000	3	4.55	***
0.50000	0.75000	2	3.03	**
0.75000	1.00000	6	9.09	******
1.00000	1.25000	2	3.03	**
1.25000	1.50000	2	3.03	**
1.50000	1.75000	1	1.52	*
1.75000	2.00000	2	3.03	**
2.00000	2.25000	3	4.55	***
2.25000	2.50000	1	1.52	*
2.50000	2.75000	0	0.00	
2.75000	3.00000	0	0.00	
3.00000	3.25000	1	1.52	*

Manifest Variable Equations

```
INFO     =    2.2125*F1      +  1.0000 E1
Std Err       0.2012 X1
t Value      10.9970
COMP     =    2.0481*F1      +  1.0000 E2
```

```
              Std Err       0.2115 X2
              t Value       9.6817
              ARITH    =    1.3036*F1     +  1.0000 E3
              Std Err       0.1730 X3
              t Value       7.5336
              SIMIL    =    2.2385*F1     +  1.0000 E4
              Std Err       0.2258 X4
              t Value       9.9114
              VOCAB    =    2.2569*F1     +  1.0000 E5
              Std Err       0.2016 X5
              t Value      11.1926
              DIGIT    =    1.0558*F1     +  1.0000 E6
              Std Err       0.2132 X6
              t Value       4.9524
              PICTCOMP =    1.7470*F2     +  1.0000 E7
              Std Err       0.2438 X7
              t Value       7.1664
              PARANG   =    1.2568*F2     +  1.0000 E8
              Std Err       0.2258 X8
              t Value       5.5665
              BLOCK    =    1.8512*F2     +  1.0000 E9
              Std Err       0.2234 X9
              t Value       8.2869
              OBJECT   =    1.6092*F2     +  1.0000 E10
              Std Err       0.2373 X10
              t Value       6.7805
              CODING   =    0.2076*F2     +  1.0000 E11
              Std Err       0.2559 X11
              t Value       0.8113
```

Variances of Exogenous Variables

Variable	Parameter	Estimate	Standard Error	t Value
F1		1.00000		
F2		1.00000		
E1	X12	3.58621	0.51128	7.01
E2	X13	4.59854	0.59010	7.79
E3	X14	3.62254	0.42385	8.55
E4	X15	5.12482	0.66730	7.68
E5	X16	3.50723	0.51079	6.87
E6	X17	6.19783	0.68634	9.03
E7	X18	5.55764	0.76388	7.28
E8	X19	5.49428	0.66400	8.27
E9	X20	3.91616	0.64564	6.07
E10	X21	5.49876	0.72562	7.58
E11	X22	8.20596	0.88155	9.31

Covariances Among Exogenous Variables

Var1	Var2	Parameter	Estimate	Standard Error	t Value
F1	F2	phi1	0.58884	0.07557	7.79

Equations with Standardized Coefficients

INFO   = 0.7597*F1   + 0.6503 E1
                  X1

COMP   = 0.6907*F1   + 0.7232 E2
                  X2

ARITH   = 0.5651*F1   + 0.8250 E3
                  X3

SIMIL   = 0.7031*F1   + 0.7111 E4
                  X4

VOCAB   = 0.7696*F1   + 0.6386 E5
                  X5

DIGIT   = 0.3904*F1   + 0.9206 E6
                  X6

PICTCOMP = 0.5954*F2   + 0.8034 E7
                  X7

PARANG   = 0.4725*F2   + 0.8813 E8
                  X8

BLOCK   = 0.6832*F2   + 0.7303 E9
                  X9

OBJECT   = 0.5658*F2   + 0.8245 E10
                  X10

CODING   = 0.0723*F2   + 0.9974 E11
                  X11

Squared Multiple Correlations

	Variable	Error Variance	Total Variance	R-Square
1	INFO	3.58621	8.48131	0.5772
2	COMP	4.59854	8.79310	0.4770
3	ARITH	3.62254	5.32184	0.3193
4	SIMIL	5.12482	10.13550	0.4944
5	VOCAB	3.50723	8.60085	0.5922
6	DIGIT	6.19783	7.31251	0.1524
7	PICTCOMP	5.55764	8.60966	0.3545
8	PARANG	5.49428	7.07389	0.2233
9	BLOCK	3.91616	7.34319	0.4667
10	OBJECT	5.49876	8.08821	0.3202
11	CODING	8.20596	8.24906	0.00522

Correlations Among Exogenous Variables

Var1	Var2	Parameter	Estimate
F1	F2	phi1	0.58884

Predicted Moments of Latent Variables

	F1	F2
F1	1.000000000	0.588837121
F2	0.588837121	1.000000000

Predicted Moments between Manifest and Latent Variables

	F1	F2
INFO	2.212487370	1.302794694
COMP	2.048063074	1.205975565
ARITH	1.303569878	0.767590334
SIMIL	2.238454947	1.318085367
VOCAB	2.256906035	1.328950053
DIGIT	1.055784414	0.621685055
PICTCOMP	1.028699882	1.747002429
PARANG	0.740066612	1.256827372
BLOCK	1.090069021	1.851223338
OBJECT	0.947543388	1.609177400
CODING	0.122244496	0.207603243

Latent Variable Score Regression Coefficients

		F1	F2
INFO	Information	0.0925174040	0.0224251784
COMP	Comprehension	0.0667885487	0.0161887932
ARITH	Arithmetic	0.0539634018	0.0130801218
SIMIL	Similarities	0.0655010813	0.0158767256
VOCAB	Vocabulary	0.0965001758	0.0233905575
DIGIT	Digit span	0.0255454894	0.0061919394
PICTCOMP	Picture completion	0.0114260073	0.0873001144
PARANG	Picture arrangement	0.0083148866	0.0635296769
BLOCK	Block design	0.0171826389	0.1312835097
OBJECT	Object Assembly	0.0106372781	0.0812738495
CODING	Coding	0.0009195931	0.0070261273

Total Effects of Exogenous on Endogenous Variables

	F1	F2
INFO	2.212487370	0.000000000
COMP	2.048063074	0.000000000
ARITH	1.303569878	0.000000000
SIMIL	2.238454947	0.000000000
VOCAB	2.256906035	0.000000000
DIGIT	1.055784414	0.000000000
PICTCOMP	0.000000000	1.747002429
PARANG	0.000000000	1.256827372
BLOCK	0.000000000	1.851223338
OBJECT	0.000000000	1.609177400
CODING	0.000000000	0.207603243

```
           Rank Order of the 5 Largest Lagrange Multipliers in _GAMMA_

                                        Lagrange        Pr >
                 Row        Column      Multiplier    Lagrange

                 COMP       F2          9.76696       0.0018
                 INFO       F2          4.45107       0.0349
                 SIMIL      F2          2.55559       0.1099
                 DIGIT      F2          1.85203       0.1735
                 PICTCOMP   F1          1.76312       0.1842

                       Stepwise Multivariate Wald Test

                  ------Cumulative Statistics-----   --Univariate Increment--
      Parameter   Chi-Square    DF    Pr > ChiSq     Chi-Square   Pr > ChiSq

      X11         0.65820       1     0.4172         0.65820      0.4172
```

Initial output interprets the instructions, followed by univariate statistics with indications of skewness and kurtosis as well as tests of multivariate kurtosis (no problem here). The full correlation matrix is provided, along with its determinant (well within bounds for avoiding multicollinearity). Note also that the convergence criterion is satisfied.

The fit indices match those of Table 14.16 in *UMS*. Standardized residuals have been omitted from *Output 14.1*, however their distribution is shown.

14.2.2 CFA Model Modification

Note that the output labeled Rank order of the 5 largest Lagrange multipliers in _GAMMA_ indicates the need for a path between COMPrehension and F2 (Performance Scale IQ). The Stepwise Multivariate Wald Test indicates the desirability of dropping X11 (the Coding subtest).

Figure 14.2 shows the batch file for accomplishing both the model modifications. This model corresponds to the final one referred to in the Results section, not to the model depicted in Table 14.20.

```
proc calis data=SASUSER.WISCSEM cov all;
   lineqs
      INFO            = X1 F1+E1,
      COMP            = X2 F1+E2 + X22  F2,
      ARITH           = X3 F1+E3,
      SIMIL           = X4 F1+E4,
      VOCAB           = X5 F1+E5,
      DIGIT           = X6 F1+E6,
      PICTCOMP        = X7 F2+E7,
      PARANG          = X8 F2+E8,
      BLOCK           = X9 F2+E9,
      OBJECT          =X10 F2+E10;
   std
      E1-E10 = X12-X21,
      F1=1,
      F2=1;
   cov
      F1 F2=phi1;
run;
```

Figure 14.2   Batch file for confirmatory factor analysis with model modifications.

Clicking on the runner icon produces *Output 14.2*.

Output 14.2   FULLY MODIFIED CONFIRMATORY FACTOR MODEL. (SELECTED OUTPUT)

Covariance Structure Analysis: Maximum Likelihood Estimation

Fit Function	0.2587
Goodness of Fit Index (GFI)	0.9518
GFI Adjusted for Degrees of Freedom (AGFI)	0.9197
Root Mean Square Residual (RMR)	0.3886
Parsimonious GFI (Mulaik, 1989)	0.6980
Chi-Square	45.0176
Chi-Square DF	33
Pr > Chi-Square	0.0792
Independence Model Chi-Square	500.35
Independence Model Chi-Square DF	45
RMSEA Estimate	0.0457
RMSEA 90% Lower Confidence Limit	.
RMSEA 90% Upper Confidence Limit	0.0766
ECVI Estimate	0.5287
ECVI 90% Lower Confidence Limit	.
ECVI 90% Upper Confidence Limit	0.6565
Probability of Close Fit	0.5553
Bentler's Comparative Fit Index	0.9736
Elliptic Corrected Chi-Square	42.7757
Pr > Elliptic Corrected Chi-Square	0.1186
Normal Theory Reweighted LS Chi-Square	44.0663
Akaike's Information Criterion	-20.9824
Bozdogan's (1987) CAIC	-158.4204
Schwarz's Bayesian Criterion	-125.4204

185

McDonald's (1989) Centrality	0.9662
Bentler & Bonett's (1980) Non-normed Index	0.9640
Bentler & Bonett's (1980) NFI	0.9100
James, Mulaik, & Brett (1982) Parsimonious NFI	0.6674
Z-Test of Wilson & Hilferty (1931)	1.4111
Bollen (1986) Normed Index Rho1	0.8773
Bollen (1988) Non-normed Index Delta2	0.9743
Hoelter's (1983) Critical N	185

Equations with Standardized Coefficients

$$INFO = 0.7770*F1 + 0.6295 \ E1$$
$$X1$$

$$COMP = 0.5043*F1 + 0.2995*F2 + 0.7037 \ E2$$
$$X2 \qquad\qquad X22$$

$$ARITH = 0.5679*F1 + 0.8231 \ E3$$
$$X3$$

$$SIMIL = 0.6948*F1 + 0.7192 \ E4$$
$$X4$$

$$VOCAB = 0.7773*F1 + 0.6291 \ E5$$
$$X5$$

$$DIGIT = 0.3984*F1 + 0.9172 \ E6$$
$$X6$$

$$PICTCOMP = 0.6176*F2 + 0.7865 \ E7$$
$$X7$$

$$PARANG = 0.4473*F2 + 0.8944 \ E8$$
$$X8$$

$$BLOCK = 0.6702*F2 + 0.7422 \ E9$$
$$X9$$

$$OBJECT = 0.5754*F2 + 0.8179 \ E10$$
$$X10$$

Squared Multiple Correlations

	Variable	Error Variance	Total Variance	R-Square
1	INFO	3.36084	8.48131	0.6037
2	COMP	4.35384	8.79310	0.5049
3	ARITH	3.60519	5.32184	0.3226
4	SIMIL	5.24325	10.13550	0.4827
5	VOCAB	3.40444	8.60085	0.6042
6	DIGIT	6.15208	7.31251	0.1587
7	PICTCOMP	5.32536	8.60966	0.3815
8	PARANG	5.65825	7.07389	0.2001
9	BLOCK	4.04499	7.34319	0.4492
10	OBJECT	5.41018	8.08821	0.3311

Correlations Among Exogenous Variables

Var1	Var2	Parameter	Estimate
F1	F2	phi1	0.53271

186

Predicted Moments of Latent Variables

	F1	F2
F1	1.000000000	0.532708931
F2	0.532708931	1.000000000

14.3　STRUCTURAL EQUATION MODEL OF HEALTH VARIABLES

Model specification is as described in Section 14.6.5 of *UMS*.

14.3.1　Model Estimation an Preliminary Evaluation

Figure 14.3 shows the batch file for the model hypothesized in Figure 14.12 in *UMS*. Note that SAS CALIS does not provide robust statistics. One might want to consider transforming the poorly distributed variables: TIMEDRS, PHYHEAL, MENHEAL, DRUGUSE, ESTEEM, CONTROL, STRESS, and ATTMAR. No transformation is done here to keep output as close as possible to that of *UMS*.

```
proc calis data=SASUSER.HLTHSEM omethod=nr cov all;
   lineqs
      ATTROLE = X1 F1 + E14,
      ESTEEM  = X2 F1 + E11,
      CONTROL = X3 F1 + E12,
      ATTMAR  = X4 F1 + E13,

      MENHEAL =  1 F2 + E7,
      PHYHEAL = X5 F2 + E6,

      TIMEDRS = 1  F3 + E5,
      DRUGUSE = X6 F3 + E8,

      SCSTRESS = X7 AGE + E21,
      F2 = X8 F1 + X9 SCSTRESS + D2,
      F3 = X10 F2 + D3;

   std
      AGE = X11,
      E5-E8 = X12-X15,
      E11-E14 = X16-X19,
      E21 = X20,
      D2-D3 = X21-X22,
      F1 = 1;

   cov
      F1 AGE = PHI1;
run;
```

Figure 14.3　Batch file for structural equation model.

Clicking on the runner icon on the toolbar produces *Output 14.3*.

Output 14.3   HYPOTHESIZED STRUCTURAL EQUATION MODEL (SELECTED OUTPUT).

The CALIS Procedure
Covariance Structure Analysis: Pattern and Initial Values

Automatic Variable Selection, the Following Manifest Variables are not Used in the Model

SUBNO   EDCODE   INCODE   EMPLMNY   STRESS   ATTMED   ATTHOUSE   ATTWORK   SEL   LTIMEDRS   LPHYHEAL

Using the VAR statement for variable selection could save memory and computing time.

LINEQS Model Statement

		Matrix	Rows	Columns	------Matrix Type-------	
Term 1	1	_SEL_	10	24	SELECTION	
	2	_BETA_	24	24	EQSBETA	IMINUSINV
	3	_GAMMA_	24	13	EQSGAMMA	
	4	_PHI_	13	13	SYMMETRIC	

The 11 Endogenous Variables

Manifest	TIMEDRS	PHYHEAL	MENHEAL	DRUGUSE	ESTEEM
	CONTROL	ATTMAR	ATTROLE	SCSTRESS	
Latent	F2	F3			

The 13 Exogenous Variables

Manifest	AGE					
Latent	F1					
Error	E14	E11	E12	E13	E7	E6
	E5	E8	E21	D2	D3	

Manifest Variable Equations

Initial Estimates

$$\text{TIMEDRS} = 1.0000 \text{ F3} + 1.0000 \text{ E5}$$
$$\text{PHYHEAL} = .*\text{F2} + 1.0000 \text{ E6}$$

188

```
                              X5
        MENHEAL  =    1.0000 F2        +   1.0000 E7
        DRUGUSE  =         .*F3        +   1.0000 E8
                              X6
        ESTEEM   =         .*F1        +   1.0000 E11
                              X2
        CONTROL  =         .*F1        +   1.0000 E12
                              X3
        ATTMAR   =         .*F1        +   1.0000 E13
                              X4
        ATTROLE  =         .*F1        +   1.0000 E14
                              X1
        SCSTRESS =         .*AGE       +   1.0000 E21
                              X7
```

Latent Variable Equations

Initial Estimates

```
F2        =        .*SCSTRESS +       .*F1       +   1.0000 D2
                   X9                 X8
F3        =        .*F2     +   1.0000 D3
                   X10
```

Variances of Exogenous Variables

Variable	Parameter	Estimate
AGE	X11	.
F1		1.00000
E14	X19	.
E11	X16	.
E12	X17	.
E13	X18	.
E7	X14	.
E6	X13	.
E5	X12	.
E8	X15	.
E21	X20	.
D2	X21	.
D3	X22	.

Covariances Among Exogenous Variables

Var1	Var2	Parameter	Estimate
AGE	F1	PHI1	.

Covariance Structure Analysis: Maximum Likelihood Estimation

Observations	445	Model Terms	1
Variables	10	Model Matrices	4
Informations	55	Parameters	23

189

		Mean	Std Dev
TIMEDRS	Visits to health professionals	7.62696629	10.10174327
PHYHEAL	Physical health symptoms	4.94382022	2.34981095
MENHEAL	Mental health symptoms	6.15056180	4.20823741
DRUGUSE	Use of psychotropic drugs	8.65617978	9.14281034
ESTEEM	Self-esteem	15.79101124	3.96821948
CONTROL	Locus-of-control	6.73707865	1.26832354
ATTMAR	Attitudes toward current marital status	22.82696629	8.92179188
ATTROLE	Attitudes toward role of women	35.19775281	6.78176506
AGE	Age in 5 year categories	4.38651685	2.22572951
SCSTRESS		2.00937079	1.30575599

		Skewness	Kurtosis
TIMEDRS	Visits to health professionals	2.884567008	9.842311580
PHYHEAL	Physical health symptoms	0.966411654	0.810382706
MENHEAL	Mental health symptoms	0.602178067	-0.286263720
DRUGUSE	Use of psychotropic drugs	1.265574453	1.058349339
ESTEEM	Self-esteem	0.507416996	0.321183293
CONTROL	Locus-of-control	0.510585868	-0.367712572
ATTMAR	Attitudes toward current marital status	0.778642618	0.858020367
ATTROLE	Attitudes toward role of women	0.044694842	-0.400541086
AGE	Age in 5 year categories	0.032389322	-1.175851290
SCSTRESS		0.769791233	0.240268561

Mardia's Multivariate Kurtosis	22.8685
Relative Multivariate Kurtosis	1.1906
Normalized Multivariate Kurtosis	15.5697
Mardia Based Kappa (Browne, 1982)	0.1906
Mean Scaled Univariate Kurtosis	0.3633
Adjusted Mean Scaled Univariate Kurtosis	0.3859

Observation Numbers with Largest Contribution to Kurtosis

164	268	39	200	265
1213	1091	971.7035	950.8789	886.6395

Covariances

		TIMEDRS	PHYHEAL	MENHEAL
TIMEDRS	Visits to health professionals	102.0452171	10.88440126	10.81755238
PHYHEAL	Physical health symptoms	10.8844013	5.52161150	4.93190100
MENHEAL	Mental health symptoms	10.8175524	4.93190100	17.70926207
DRUGUSE	Use of psychotropic drugs	26.7948780	8.89955967	14.11719810
ESTEEM	Self-esteem	0.6493420	0.73598036	3.71171677
CONTROL	Locus-of-control	0.3026015	0.34105173	1.52390930
ATTMAR	Attitudes toward current marital status	4.2528748	1.66818504	9.03962446
ATTROLE	Attitudes toward role of women	-5.5702095	-0.79517158	-2.09966090
AGE	Age in 5 year categories	-0.4928788	0.08032189	-0.85337079
SCSTRESS		3.4069269	0.92226187	2.11802288

Covariances

		DRUGUSE	ESTEEM	CONTROL
TIMEDRS	Visits to health professionals	26.79487802	0.64934204	0.302601478
PHYHEAL	Physical health symptoms	8.89955967	0.73598036	0.341051726
MENHEAL	Mental health symptoms	14.11719810	3.71171677	1.523909303
DRUGUSE	Use of psychotropic drugs	83.59098087	-1.80399838	0.810299625
ESTEEM	Self-esteem	-1.80399838	15.74676587	1.735469177
CONTROL	Locus-of-control	0.81029963	1.73546918	1.608644600
ATTMAR	Attitudes toward current marital status	6.86604920	10.54934204	2.287736613
ATTROLE	Attitudes toward role of women	-6.04672032	5.28015994	0.034092519
AGE	Age in 5 year categories	-0.71590748	0.14627493	-0.384634072
SCSTRESS		3.66041381	-0.52571738	0.107334194

Covariances

		ATTMAR	ATTROLE	AGE
TIMEDRS	Visits to health professionals	4.25287478	-5.57020954	-0.492878834
PHYHEAL	Physical health symptoms	1.66818504	-0.79517158	0.080321895
MENHEAL	Mental health symptoms	9.03962446	-2.09966090	-0.853370787
DRUGUSE	Use of psychotropic drugs	6.86604920	-6.04672032	-0.715907481
ESTEEM	Self-esteem	10.54934204	5.28015994	0.146274927
CONTROL	Locus-of-control	2.28773661	0.03409252	-0.384634072
ATTMAR	Attitudes toward current marital status	79.59837028	-4.15489422	-1.955491447
ATTROLE	Attitudes toward role of women	-4.15489422	45.99233728	3.279248912
AGE	Age in 5 year categories	-1.95549145	3.27924891	4.953871849
SCSTRESS		1.28932782	-2.12507799	-0.844395890

Covariances

		SCSTRESS
TIMEDRS	Visits to health professionals	3.406926916
PHYHEAL	Physical health symptoms	0.922261869
MENHEAL	Mental health symptoms	2.118022877
DRUGUSE	Use of psychotropic drugs	3.660413807
ESTEEM	Self-esteem	-0.525717380
CONTROL	Locus-of-control	0.107334194
ATTMAR	Attitudes toward current marital status	1.289327817
ATTROLE	Attitudes toward role of women	-2.125077994
AGE	Age in 5 year categories	-0.844395890
SCSTRESS		1.704998702

Determinant 122127617084   Ln   25.528332

Set Covariances of Exogenous Manifest Variables

AGE

Fit Function	0.3664
Goodness of Fit Index (GFI)	0.9275
GFI Adjusted for Degrees of Freedom (AGFI)	0.8754
Root Mean Square Residual (RMR)	2.4758

Parsimonious GFI (Mulaik, 1989)	0.6596
Chi-Square	162.7030
Chi-Square DF	32
Pr > Chi-Square	<.0001
Independence Model Chi-Square	744.59
Independence Model Chi-Square DF	45
RMSEA Estimate	0.0959
RMSEA 90% Lower Confidence Limit	0.0816
RMSEA 90% Upper Confidence Limit	0.1108
ECVI Estimate	0.4727
ECVI 90% Lower Confidence Limit	0.3905
ECVI 90% Upper Confidence Limit	0.5723
Probability of Close Fit	0.0000
Bentler's Comparative Fit Index	0.8132
Elliptic Corrected Chi-Square	136.6597
Pr > Elliptic Corrected Chi-Square	<.0001
Normal Theory Reweighted LS Chi-Square	173.4884
Akaike's Information Criterion	98.7030
Bozdogan's (1987) CAIC	-64.4354
Schwarz's Bayesian Criterion	-32.4354
McDonald's (1989) Centrality	0.8634
Bentler & Bonett's (1980) Non-normed Index	0.7373
Bentler & Bonett's (1980) NFI	0.7815
James, Mulaik, & Brett (1982) Parsimonious NFI	0.5557
Z-Test of Wilson & Hilferty (1931)	8.7179
Bollen (1986) Normed Index Rho1	0.6927
Bollen (1988) Non-normed Index Delta2	0.8166
Hoelter's (1983) Critical N	128

Asymptotically Standardized Residual Matrix

		TIMEDRS	PHYHEAL	MENHEAL
TIMEDRS	Visits to health professionals	-1.450518889	4.622562214	-4.761313769
PHYHEAL	Physical health symptoms	4.622562214	-1.450536075	-1.503039249
MENHEAL	Mental health symptoms	-4.761313769	-1.503039249	-1.450606343
DRUGUSE	Use of psychotropic drugs	-1.450535098	0.407356544	-0.716830440
ESTEEM	Self-esteem	-2.314111790	-2.555794631	2.327553090
CONTROL	Locus-of-control	-0.909251315	0.554540833	4.886487295
ATTMAR	Attitudes toward current marital status	-0.138580054	0.042193502	3.948065842
ATTROLE	Attitudes toward role of women	-2.273827579	-1.880607486	-2.337734512
AGE	Age in 5 year categories	1.220895457	3.058987560	0.291186646
SCSTRESS		0.087867085	-3.721096997	1.669136963

Asymptotically Standardized Residual Matrix

		DRUGUSE	ESTEEM	CONTROL
TIMEDRS	Visits to health professionals	-1.450535098	-2.314111790	-0.909251315
PHYHEAL	Physical health symptoms	0.407356544	-2.555794631	0.554540833
MENHEAL	Mental health symptoms	-0.716830440	2.327553090	4.886487295
DRUGUSE	Use of psychotropic drugs	-1.450551322	-4.331238220	0.035643353
ESTEEM	Self-esteem	-4.331238220	0.000000000	-1.679100014
CONTROL	Locus-of-control	0.035643353	-1.679100014	0.000000000
ATTMAR	Attitudes toward current marital status	0.600436260	0.035867639	1.043106403
ATTROLE	Attitudes toward role of women	-2.672871488	4.408109260	-2.048661289

192

| AGE | Age in 5 year categories | 1.065584185 | 1.715530269 | -3.312709740 |
| SCSTRESS | | 1.054531555 | -2.286764367 | 1.347656983 |

Asymptotically Standardized Residual Matrix

		ATTMAR	ATTROLE	AGE
TIMEDRS	Visits to health professionals	-0.138580054	-2.273827579	1.220895457
PHYHEAL	Physical health symptoms	0.042193502	-1.880607486	3.058987560
MENHEAL	Mental health symptoms	3.948065842	-2.337734512	0.291186646
DRUGUSE	Use of psychotropic drugs	0.600436260	-2.672871488	1.065584185
ESTEEM	Self-esteem	0.035867639	4.408109260	1.715530269
CONTROL	Locus-of-control	1.043106403	-2.048661289	-3.312709740
ATTMAR	Attitudes toward current marital status	0.000000000	-3.391796834	-2.233892894
ATTROLE	Attitudes toward role of women	-3.391796834	0.000000000	4.735323197
AGE	Age in 5 year categories	-2.233892894	4.735323197	0.000000000
SCSTRESS		2.323696051	-5.080275073	0.000000000

		SCSTRESS
TIMEDRS	Visits to health professionals	0.087867085
PHYHEAL	Physical health symptoms	-3.721096997
MENHEAL	Mental health symptoms	1.669136963
DRUGUSE	Use of psychotropic drugs	1.054531555
ESTEEM	Self-esteem	-2.286764367
CONTROL	Locus-of-control	1.347656983
ATTMAR	Attitudes toward current marital status	2.323696051
ATTROLE	Attitudes toward role of women	-5.080275073
AGE	Age in 5 year categories	0.000000000
SCSTRESS		0.000000000

Average Standardized Residual	1.797901
Average Off-diagonal Standardized Residual	2.068497

Rank Order of the 10 Largest Asymptotically Standardized Residuals

Row	Column	Residual
SCSTRESS	ATTROLE	-5.08028
CONTROL	MENHEAL	4.88649
MENHEAL	TIMEDRS	-4.76131
AGE	ATTROLE	4.73532
PHYHEAL	TIMEDRS	4.62256
ATTROLE	ESTEEM	4.40811
ESTEEM	DRUGUSE	-4.33124
ATTMAR	MENHEAL	3.94807
SCSTRESS	PHYHEAL	-3.72110
ATTROLE	ATTMAR	-3.39180

193

Distribution of Asymptotically Standardized Residuals

Each * Represents 1 Residuals

---------Range---------		Freq	Percent	
-5.25000	-5.00000	1	1.82	*
-5.00000	-4.75000	1	1.82	*
-4.75000	-4.50000	0	0.00	
-4.50000	-4.25000	1	1.82	*
-4.25000	-4.00000	0	0.00	
-4.00000	-3.75000	0	0.00	
-3.75000	-3.50000	1	1.82	*
-3.50000	-3.25000	2	3.64	**
-3.25000	-3.00000	0	0.00	
-3.00000	-2.75000	0	0.00	
-2.75000	-2.50000	2	3.64	**
-2.50000	-2.25000	4	7.27	****
-2.25000	-2.00000	2	3.64	**
-2.00000	-1.75000	1	1.82	*
-1.75000	-1.50000	2	3.64	**
-1.50000	-1.25000	5	9.09	*****
-1.25000	-1.00000	0	0.00	
-1.00000	-0.75000	1	1.82	*
-0.75000	-0.50000	1	1.82	*
-0.50000	-0.25000	0	0.00	
-0.25000	0	1	1.82	*
0	0.25000	11	20.00	***********
0.25000	0.50000	2	3.64	**
0.50000	0.75000	2	3.64	**
0.75000	1.00000	0	0.00	
1.00000	1.25000	4	7.27	****
1.25000	1.50000	1	1.82	*
1.50000	1.75000	2	3.64	**
1.75000	2.00000	0	0.00	
2.00000	2.25000	0	0.00	
2.25000	2.50000	2	3.64	**
2.50000	2.75000	0	0.00	
2.75000	3.00000	0	0.00	
3.00000	3.25000	1	1.82	*
3.25000	3.50000	0	0.00	
3.50000	3.75000	0	0.00	
3.75000	4.00000	1	1.82	*
4.00000	4.25000	0	0.00	
4.25000	4.50000	1	1.82	*
4.50000	4.75000	2	3.64	**
4.75000	5.00000	1	1.82	*

Rank Order of the 8 Largest Lagrange Multipliers in _GAMMA_

Row	Column	Lagrange Multiplier	Pr > Lagrange
MENHEAL	F1	29.69123	<.0001
ATTROLE	AGE	22.42295	<.0001

194

F3	F1	17.26270	<.0001
DRUGUSE	F1	11.13652	0.0008
CONTROL	AGE	10.97478	0.0009
PHYHEAL	AGE	8.25116	0.0041
F2	AGE	5.06393	0.0244
ATTMAR	AGE	4.99067	0.0255

Stepwise Multivariate Wald Test

	------Cumulative Statistics-----			--Univariate Increment--	
Parameter	Chi-Square	DF	Pr > ChiSq	Chi-Square	Pr > ChiSq
PHI1	0.04892	1	0.8249	0.04892	0.8249
X22	0.17734	2	0.9151	0.12841	0.7201

14.3.2 Model Modification

Note that the model fit differs a bit from that in *UMS* because of the difference in estimation techniques (lack of robust estimation here). The suggestion of a path between F1 (Poor Sense of Self) and MENHEAL appears in the output under Rank order of 8 largest Lagrange multipliers in _GAMMA_.

Output 14.4 shows the results of adding a path from F1 to MENHEAL (MENHEAL = 1 F2 + X38 F1 + E7).

Output 14.4 GOODNESS OF FIT INFORMATION AFTER ADDITION OF MENTAL HEALTH PREDICTED BY POOR SENSE OF SELF.

The CALIS Procedure
Covariance Structure Analysis: Maximum Likelihood Estimation

Fit Function	0.2873
Goodness of Fit Index (GFI)	0.9424
GFI Adjusted for Degrees of Freedom (AGFI)	0.8978
Root Mean Square Residual (RMR)	2.0426
Parsimonious GFI (Mulaik, 1989)	0.6492
Chi-Square	127.5501
Chi-Square DF	31
Pr > Chi-Square	<.0001
Independence Model Chi-Square	744.59
Independence Model Chi-Square DF	45
RMSEA Estimate	0.0838

RMSEA 90% Lower Confidence Limit	0.0690
RMSEA 90% Upper Confidence Limit	0.0991
ECVI Estimate	0.3981
ECVI 90% Lower Confidence Limit	0.3274
ECVI 90% Upper Confidence Limit	0.4863
Probability of Close Fit	0.0001
Bentler's Comparative Fit Index	0.8620
Elliptic Corrected Chi-Square	107.1336
Pr > Elliptic Corrected Chi-Square	<.0001
Normal Theory Reweighted LS Chi-Square	135.6379
Akaike's Information Criterion	65.5501
Bozdogan's (1987) CAIC	-92.4902
Schwarz's Bayesian Criterion	-61.4902
McDonald's (1989) Centrality	0.8972
Bentler & Bonett's (1980) Non-normed Index	0.7997
Bentler & Bonett's (1980) NFI	0.8287
James, Mulaik, & Brett (1982) Parsimonious NFI	0.5709
Z-Test of Wilson & Hilferty (1931)	7.1997
Bollen (1986) Normed Index Rho1	0.7513
Bollen (1988) Non-normed Index Delta2	0.8647
Hoelter's (1983) Critical N	158

WARNING: The central parameter matrix _PHI_ has probably 1 negative eigenvalue(s).

Variances of Exogenous Variables

Variable	Parameter	Estimate	Standard Error	t Value
AGE	X11	4.95387	0.33248	14.90
F1		1.00000		
E14	X19	45.56045	3.07572	14.81
E11	X16	9.27988	1.14248	8.12
E12	X17	1.13137	0.10615	10.66
E13	X18	64.29115	5.09612	12.62
E7	X14	8.09402	0.84971	9.53
E6	X13	2.45534	0.28027	8.76
E5	X12	74.63226	6.18644	12.06
E8	X15	57.40024	5.18403	11.07
E21	X20	1.56107	0.10477	14.90
D2	X21	4.84866	0.80213	6.04
D3	X22	-1.00581	3.81717	-0.26

Rank Order of the 7 Largest Lagrange Multipliers in _GAMMA_

Row	Column	Lagrange Multiplier	Pr > Lagrange
ATTROLE	AGE	23.26811	<.0001
ESTEEM	AGE	7.19830	0.0073
PHYHEAL	AGE	7.17804	0.0074
CONTROL	AGE	6.82775	0.0090
F2	AGE	6.71862	0.0095

```
PHYHEAL    F1              4.63544    0.0313
F3         F1              4.63478    0.0313
```

SAS CALIS indicates the problem of negative variance for D3 by the warning message following the goodness of fit output, and then shows a negative parameter estimates in the table labeled Variances of Exogenous Variables. The desirability of adding a path between ATTROLE and AGE is shown in the last portion of *Output 14.4*.

Output 14.5 shows the output regarding correlated errors after adding a path between ATTROLE and AGE (ATTROLE = X1 F1 + E14 + X24 AGE).

Output 14.5   EDITED OUTPUT FOR UNIVARIATE LM TEST FOR ADDING CORRELATED ERRORS.

```
        Rank Order of the 10 Largest Lagrange Multipliers in _PHI_

                                    Lagrange        Pr >
            Row         Column      Multiplier      Lagrange

            E5          E6          18.45769        <.0001
            E5          E7          17.83499        <.0001
            E11         E14         16.87286        <.0001
            E21         E14         16.23134        <.0001
            D2          E7          13.90394        0.0002
            D3          E6          13.90377        0.0002
            D2          E6          13.89712        0.0002
            D3          E7          13.89333        0.0002
            E21         E7          12.73494        0.0004
            E21         E11         10.10111        0.0015
```

These values differ from those in *UMS*, and would suggest correlated errors between TIMEDRS and MENHEAL in addition to those between ATTROLE and ESTEEM and between TIMEDRS and PHYHEAL. To keep results as close as possible to those in *UMS*, however, subsequent runs correlate only the latter two sets of errors.

Figure 14.4 shows the batch file of instructions for the final model.

197

```
proc calis data=SASUSER.HLTHSEM omethod=nr cov all;
   lineqs
      ATTROLE = X1 F1 + E14 + X46 AGE,
      ESTEEM  = X2 F1 + E11,
      CONTROL = X3 F1 + E12,
      ATTMAR  = X4 F1 + E13,

      MENHEAL = 1  F2 + X38  F1 + E7,
      PHYHEAL = X5 F2 + E6,

      TIMEDRS = 1  F3 + E5,
      DRUGUSE = X6 F3 + E8,

      SCSTRESS = X7 AGE + E21,
      F2 = X8 F1 + X9 SCSTRESS + D2,
      F3 = X10 F2 + D3;

   std
      AGE = X11,
      E5-E8 = X12-X15,
      E11-E14 = X16-X19,
      E21 = X20,
      D2-D3 = X21-X22,
      F1 = 1;

   cov
      F1 AGE = PHI1,
      E14 E11 = PHI2,
      E5 E6 = PHI3;
run;
```

Figure 14.4   Batch file for final structural equation model.

Clicking on the runner icon on the toolbar produces *Output 14.6.*

Output 14.6   FINAL STRUCTURAL EQUATION MODEL.

Covariance Structure Analysis: Maximum Likelihood Estimation

Fit Function	0.1556
Goodness of Fit Index (GFI)	0.9704
GFI Adjusted for Degrees of Freedom (AGFI)	0.9418
Root Mean Square Residual (RMR)	1.4194
Parsimonious GFI (Mulaik, 1989)	0.6038
Chi-Square	69.0643
Chi-Square DF	28
Pr > Chi-Square	<.0001
Independence Model Chi-Square	744.59
Independence Model Chi-Square DF	45
RMSEA Estimate	0.0575

RMSEA 90% Lower Confidence Limit	0.0405
RMSEA 90% Upper Confidence Limit	0.0747
ECVI Estimate	0.2803
ECVI 90% Lower Confidence Limit	0.2334
ECVI 90% Upper Confidence Limit	0.3449
Probability of Close Fit	0.2193
Bentler's Comparative Fit Index	0.9413
Elliptic Corrected Chi-Square	58.0094
Pr > Elliptic Corrected Chi-Square	0.0007
Normal Theory Reweighted LS Chi-Square	67.7582
Akaike's Information Criterion	13.0643
Bozdogan's (1987) CAIC	-129.6818
Schwarz's Bayesian Criterion	-101.6818
McDonald's (1989) Centrality	0.9549
Bentler & Bonett's (1980) Non-normed Index	0.9057
Bentler & Bonett's (1980) NFI	0.9072
James, Mulaik, & Brett (1982) Parsimonious NFI	0.5645
Z-Test of Wilson & Hilferty (1931)	4.0306
Bollen (1986) Normed Index Rho1	0.8509
Bollen (1988) Non-normed Index Delta2	0.9427
Hoelter's (1983) Critical N	267

Manifest Variable Equations

```
TIMEDRS  =   1.0000 F3      +  1.0000 E5
PHYHEAL  =   0.5726*F2      +  1.0000 E6
Std Err      0.0597 X5
t Value      9.5924


MENHEAL  =   1.0000 F2      +  1.3957*F1      +  1.0000 E7
Std Err                        0.2346 X38
t Value                        5.9503
DRUGUSE  =   1.2753*F3      +  1.0000 E8
Std Err      0.2047 X6
t Value      6.2303
ESTEEM   =   2.4581*F1      +  1.0000 E11
Std Err      0.2488 X2
t Value      9.8798
CONTROL  =   0.6898*F1      +  1.0000 E12
Std Err      0.0765 X3
t Value      9.0144
ATTMAR   =   4.0817*F1      +  1.0000 E13
Std Err      0.5293 X4
t Value      7.7108
ATTROLE  =   0.5872*AGE     +-0.00627*F1     +  1.0000 E14
Std Err      0.1399 X46        0.4509 X1
t Value      4.1985            -0.0139
SCSTRESS =  -0.1705*AGE     +  1.0000 E21
Std Err      0.0266 X7
t Value     -6.3981
```

Latent Variable Equations

```
F2        =    1.0998*SCSTRESS  +   0.4105*F1       +  1.0000 D2
Std Err        0.1250 X9            0.2101 X8
t Value        8.7972               1.9538
F3        =    1.4518*F2        +   1.0000 D3
Std Err        0.2365 X10
t Value        6.1392
```

Variances of Exogenous Variables

Variable	Parameter	Estimate	Standard Error	t Value
AGE	X11	4.95387	0.33248	14.90
F1		1.00000		
E14	X19	43.84922	2.94297	14.90
E11	X16	9.70469	1.10795	8.76
E12	X17	1.13288	0.10511	10.78
E13	X18	62.93849	5.08129	12.39
E7	X14	6.71648	0.89989	7.46
E6	X13	2.98654	0.30070	9.93
E5	X12	81.66470	6.39234	12.78
E8	X15	50.73696	6.41015	7.92
E21	X20	1.56107	0.10477	14.90
D2	X21	5.45372	0.90153	6.05
D3	X22	3.90186	2.83655	1.38

Covariances Among Exogenous Variables

Var1	Var2	Parameter	Estimate	Standard Error	t Value
AGE	F1	PHI1	-0.21993	0.13475	-1.63
E14	E11	PHI2	5.20966	1.27814	4.08
E6	E5	PHI3	4.39530	1.05751	4.16

Equations with Standardized Coefficients

```
TIMEDRS  =    0.4450 F3     +   0.8955 E5
PHYHEAL  =    0.6772*F2     +   0.7358 E6
              X5
MENHEAL  =    0.6614 F2     +   0.3323*F1    +  0.6170 E7
                                  X38
DRUGUSE  =    0.6266*F3     +   0.7793 E8
              X6
ESTEEM   =    0.6194*F1     +   0.7850 E11
              X2
CONTROL  =    0.5438*F1     +   0.8392 E12
              X3
ATTMAR   =    0.4575*F1     +   0.8892 E13
              X4
```

200

```
ATTROLE   =   0.1936*AGE        +-0.00093*F1       +  0.9811 E14
                X46                     X1
SCSTRESS  =  -0.2905*AGE        +  0.9569 E21
                X7
```

Latent Variable Equations

```
F2       =   0.5169*SCSTRESS +  0.1478*F1       +  0.8406 D2
                X9                   X8
F3       =   0.8981*F2       +  0.4398 D3
                X10
```

Squared Multiple Correlations

	Variable	Error Variance	Total Variance	R-Square
1	TIMEDRS	81.66470	101.83365	0.1981
2	PHYHEAL	2.98654	5.51673	0.4586
3	MENHEAL	6.71648	17.64374	0.6193
4	DRUGUSE	50.73696	83.53994	0.3927
5	ESTEEM	9.70469	15.74677	0.3837
6	CONTROL	1.13288	1.60864	0.2958
7	ATTMAR	62.93849	79.59837	0.2093
8	ATTROLE	43.84922	45.55927	0.0375
9	SCSTRESS	1.56107	1.70500	0.0844
10	F2	5.45372	7.71836	0.2934
11	F3	3.90186	20.16895	0.8065

Correlations Among Exogenous Variables

Var1	Var2	Parameter	Estimate
AGE	F1	PHI1	-0.09881
E14	E11	PHI2	0.25254
E6	E5	PHI3	0.28144

Predicted Moments of Latent Variables

	F2	F3	F1
F2	7.71835772	11.20514335	0.451771600
F3	11.20514335	20.16895350	0.655860446
F1	0.45177160	0.65586045	1.000000000

201

Predicted Moments between Manifest and Latent Variables

	F2	F3	F1
TIMEDRS	11.20514335	20.16895350	0.655860446
PHYHEAL	4.41915063	6.41551197	0.258662117
MENHEAL	8.34887632	12.12050016	1.847429491
DRUGUSE	14.29000454	25.72161979	0.836423815
ESTEEM	1.11048301	1.61214624	2.458062914
CONTROL	0.31161359	0.45238573	0.689759136
ATTMAR	1.84397405	2.67699351	4.081651104
ATTROLE	-0.60120432	-0.87279974	-0.135421198
AGE	-1.01894585	-1.47925695	-0.219933649
SCSTRESS	1.89052192	2.74456950	0.037488065

Latent Variable Score Regression Coefficients

		F2	F3	F1
TIMEDRS	Visits to health professionals	0.0114277882	0.0586075513	-.0005648918
PHYHEAL	Physical health symptoms	0.3680959860	0.4028265160	-.0181955062
MENHEAL	Mental health symptoms	0.2783116793	0.3536280681	0.0637538006
DRUGUSE	Use of psychotropic drugs	0.0641245855	0.1648073276	-.0031697691
ESTEEM	Self-esteem	-.0268587600	-.0341272469	0.1022741680
CONTROL	Locus-of-control	-.0604277712	-.0767806656	0.2300999759
ATTMAR	Attitudes toward current marital status	-.0064363756	-.0081781802	0.0245087620
ATTROLE	Attitudes toward role of women	0.0032052278	0.0040726229	-.0122050315
AGE	Age in 5 year categories	0.0025674312	0.0032622265	-.0097763966
SCSTRESS		0.4131035282	0.5248971332	-.0513019436

Total Effects of Exogenous on Endogenous Variables

	AGE	F1	SCSTRESS	F2	F3
TIMEDRS	-.2721457316	0.596006442	1.596614922	1.451752272	1.000000000
PHYHEAL	-.1073304413	0.235056542	0.629682425	0.572550637	0.000000000
MENHEAL	-.1874601727	1.806200692	1.099784690	1.000000000	0.000000000
DRUGUSE	-.3470695213	0.760091549	2.036175153	1.851430714	1.275307605
ESTEEM	0.0000000000	2.458062914	0.000000000	0.000000000	0.000000000
CONTROL	0.0000000000	0.689759136	0.000000000	0.000000000	0.000000000
ATTMAR	0.0000000000	4.081651104	0.000000000	0.000000000	0.000000000
ATTROLE	0.5872477714	-0.006265653	0.000000000	0.000000000	0.000000000
SCSTRESS	-.1704517024	0.000000000	0.000000000	0.000000000	0.000000000
F2	-.1874601727	0.410542800	1.099784690	0.000000000	0.000000000
F3	-.2721457316	0.596006442	1.596614922	1.451752272	0.000000000

Indirect Effects of Exogenous on Endogenous Variables

	AGE	F1	SCSTRESS	F2	F3
TIMEDRS	-.2721457316	0.5960064424	1.596614922	1.451752272	0
PHYHEAL	-.1073304413	0.2350565416	0.629682425	0.000000000	0
MENHEAL	-.1874601727	0.4105427999	1.099784690	0.000000000	0
DRUGUSE	-.3470695213	0.7600915489	2.036175153	1.851430714	0
ESTEEM	0.0000000000	0.0000000000	0.000000000	0.000000000	0

CONTROL	0.0000000000	0.0000000000	0.000000000	0.000000000	0
ATTMAR	0.0000000000	0.0000000000	0.000000000	0.000000000	0
ATTROLE	0.0000000000	0.0000000000	0.000000000	0.000000000	0
SCSTRESS	0.0000000000	0.0000000000	0.000000000	0.000000000	0
F2	-.1874601727	0.0000000000	0.000000000	0.000000000	0
F3	-.2721457316	0.5960064424	1.596614922	0.000000000	0

Stepwise Multivariate Wald Test

	------Cumulative Statistics-----			--Univariate Increment--	
Parameter	Chi-Square	DF	Pr > ChiSq	Chi-Square	Pr > ChiSq
X1	0.0001931	1	0.9889	0.0001931	0.9889
X22	1.89238	2	0.3882	1.89218	0.1690
PHI1	4.57373	3	0.2058	2.68135	0.1015
X8	8.25740	4	0.0826	3.68367	0.0549

The results of the Wald test (end of output) are similar to those of Table 14.28 in *UMS*. The parameter X1, representing the path between ATTROLE and F1, can be dropped without harming the model. Also unnecessary is X22 (the D3 parameter), as well as the path represented by PHI1 (the correlation between AGE and F1). In addition, the SAS results suggest that X8 (the path between F1 and F2) is not critical to the model.

Chapter 15. Survival/Failure Analysis

This chapter demonstrates survival analysis using SAS for Windows, for the complete example of Chapter 15 in *UMS*. The file to use is SURVIVAL.SAS7BDAT.

Differences in survival time following treatment with either an experimental drug or a placebo are examined in the 312 cases who participated in the trial. Additional covariates age (in days), serum bilirubin in mg/dl, serum albumin in gm/dl, prothrombin time in seconds, and presence of edema. Edema has three levels treated as continuous: 1) no edema and no diuretic therapy for edema, coded 0.00; 2) edema present without diuretics or edema resolved by diuretics, coded 0.50; and 3) edema despite diuretic therapy, coded 1.00. Coding for status is 0 = censored, 1 = liver transplant, and 2 = event.

15.1   EVALUATION OF ASSUMPTIONS

Procedures of Section 4.1.1 are used to evaluate accuracy of input, adequacy of sample size, missing data, distributions and univariate outliers. Logarithmic transform of bilirubin follows the procedures shown in Section 4.1.5. The new variable, LBILIRUB, is added to the data set, which is saved as SURVIVE1. However, a transformation that requires dividing a variable by a constant is not available in **Interactive Data Analysis**. Therefore, the transformation is done by typing the syntax of Figure 15.1 into the **Program Editor**. The transformed variable, Y_AGE is added to the data set, which is saved as SURVIVET.SAS7BDAT, a portion of which is shown in Figure 15.2.

```
Program Editor - survxform
data SASUSER.SURVIVET;
  set SASUSER.SURVIVE1;
  Y_AGE = AGE/365.25;
run;
```

Figure 15.1   Batch file to create transformation of AGE.

	SGOT	TRIGLIC	PLATELET	PROTHOM	STAGE	LBILIRUB	Y_AGE
1	137.95	172	190	12.2	4	1.1614	58.7652
2	113.52	88	221	10.6	3	0.0414	56.4463
3	96.10	55	151	12.0	4	0.1461	70.0726
4	60.63	92	183	10.3	4	0.2553	54.7406
5	113.15	72	136	10.9	3	0.5315	38.1054
6	93.00	63	.	11.0	3	-0.0969	66.2587
7	60.45	213	204	9.7	3	0.0000	55.5346
8	28.38	189	373	11.0	3	-0.5229	53.0568
9	144.15	88	251	11.0	2	0.5051	42.5079
10	147.25	143	302	11.5	4	1.1004	70.5599
11	79.05	79	258	12.0	4	0.1461	53.7139
12	82.15	95	71	13.6	4	0.5563	59.1376
13	88.35	130	244	10.6	3	-0.1549	45.6893
14	71.00	.	156	11.0	4	-0.0969	56.2218
15	127.71	96	295	11.0	3	-0.0969	64.6461

Figure 15.2 Portion of SASUSER.SURVIVET showing transformed variables: LBILIRUB and Y_AGE.

Multivariate outliers and multicollinearity are evaluated through regression using the procedures of Section 4.1.6 and 4.1.7. The file is saved (as SURVNEW) with the three outliers deleted (ID = 191, 107, and 14).

Differences between withdrawn (censored) and remaining cases are evaluated through standard multiple regression after creating a dummy variable, XPLANT . Creating the dummy variable is most easily done through the syntax of Figure 15.3, in which the new variable is added to the data set and temporarily saved in a file: WORK:SURVWITH. Then standard multiple regression is run as per Figures 4.26 through 4.28, selecting XPLANT as the **Dependent:** variable and ALBUMIN, DRUG, EDEMA, PROTHOM, LBILIRUB, and Y_AGE as **Independent:** variables. The minimum number of columns specified is 6, forcing all covariates into the regression. This produces *Output 15.1.*

Output 15.1 PARTIAL OUTPUT FROM STANDARD MULTIPLE REGRESSION FOR DIFFERENCES BETWEEN LIVER TRANSPLANT AND REMAINING CASES.

Dependent Variable: XPLANT

First 6 Vars Entered: R-Square = 0.0641 and C(p) = 7.0000

Analysis of Variance

Source	DF	Sum of Squares	Mean Square	F Value	Pr > F
Model	6	1.14358	0.19060	3.45	0.0026
Error	302	16.68813	0.05526		
Corrected Total	308	17.83172			

Variable	Parameter Estimate	Standard Error	Type II SS	F Value	Pr > F
Intercept	0.53572	0.24261	0.26943	4.88	0.0280
* DRUG	-0.01794	0.02711	0.02419	0.44	0.5087
* EDEMA	-0.01521	0.05967	0.00359	0.06	0.7989
* ALBUMIN	0.00607	0.03702	0.00149	0.03	0.8698
* PROTHOM	-0.02455	0.01726	0.11177	2.02	0.1560
* LBILIRUB	0.07528	0.03512	0.25382	4.59	0.0329
* Y_AGE	-0.00448	0.00134	0.62063	11.23	0.0009

Recoding is required because it is decided to combine liver transplant cases with other censored cases. Figure 15.3 shows the syntax to accomplish the recoding, so that for the remaining analyses all censored cases (including liver transplant) are coded 0 and non-survivors retain the code of 2. The final recoded data set is saved as SURVFINL.

```
Program Editor - survival recode.sas
data SASUSER.SURVFINL;
  set SASUSER.SURVNEW;
  if STATUS = 1 then STATUS = 0;
run;
```

Figure 15.3   Batch file to recode
censored cases.

Proportionality of hazards is tested by creating interactions between survival time (days) and the various covariates. The syntax of Figure 15.4 shows the syntax for creation of the interactions within the PHREG run to test the assumption.

```
Program Editor - survival prop.sas
proc phreg data=SASUSER.SURVFINL;
  model days*status(0) = albumin edema prothom lbilirub y_age
    drug alb_int ede_int pro_int lbil_int age_int drug_int;
  alb_int = albumin*log(days);
  ede_int = edema*log(days);
  pro_int = prothom*log(days);
  lbil_int = lbilirub*log(days);
  age_int = y_age*log(days);
  drug_int = drug*log(days);
run;
```

Figure 15.4   Creation of covariate by time interactions and
test of proportionality of hazards.

This produces *Output 15.2* which, like Table 15.21 of *UMS* shows no serious violation of proportionality of hazards with α = .008.

Output 15.2   SELECTED OUTPUT FOR TEST OF PROPORTIONALITY OF HAZARDS.

```
                        The PHREG Procedure
                 Analysis of Maximum Likelihood Estimates

               Parameter    Standard     Wald                   Hazard
Variable   DF   Estimate      Error    Chi-Square  Pr > ChiSq    Ratio    Variable Label

ALBUMIN    1   -1.82117     1.89162     0.9269      0.3357       0.162
EDEMA      1    5.68403     2.38994     5.6564      0.0174     294.132
PROTHOM    1    1.44921     0.73358     3.9027      0.0482       4.260
LBILIRUB   1   -0.37125     1.81525     0.0418      0.8380       0.690    log10( BILIRUBI )
Y_AGE      1    0.08727     0.07515     1.3483      0.2456       1.091
DRUG       1    2.37919     1.38215     2.9631      0.0852      10.796
alb_int    1    0.12918     0.27177     0.2259      0.6346       1.138
ede_int    1   -0.77775     0.36390     4.5679      0.0326       0.459
pro_int    1   -0.16417     0.10627     2.3864      0.1224       0.849
lbil_int   1    0.33924     0.26090     1.6907      0.1935       1.404
age_int    1   -0.00784     0.01065     0.5420      0.4616       0.992
drug_int   1   -0.31939     0.19669     2.6367      0.1044       0.727
```

Figure 15.5 shows syntax for assessing multicollinearity using SAS FACTOR to produce SMCs, which are in *Output 15.3*.

```
proc FACTOR data=SASUSER.SURVFINL prior= smc;
   var albumin drug edema prothom lbilirub y_age;
run;
```

Figure 15.5   Batch file for producing SMCs through PROC FACTOR.

Output 15.3   SELECTED FACTOR ANALYSIS OUTPUT SHOWING SMCs TO EVALUATE MULTICOLLINEARITY.

```
                       The FACTOR Procedure
              Initial Factor Method: Principal Factors

                 Prior Communality Estimates: SMC

     ALBUMIN        DRUG         EDEMA       PROTHOM      LBILIRUB        Y_AGE

   0.23890758    0.02584870    0.31379624   0.26557461   0.26391098    0.10544499
```

15.2 COX REGRESSION SURVIVAL ANALYSIS

SAS PHREG does sequential survival analysis by having variables enter singly on each step. The syntax of Figure 15.6 requests FORWARD selection with variables forced to enter even though significance to enter is only $p \le .50$. The SEQUENTIAL instruction forces variables to be added to the model in the order specified in the MODEL instruction. Thus, only the last two steps of the analysis are of interest: step 5 which all covariates are entered, and step 6 in which the IV (drug) is added to the covariates in the model. The final instruction saves predicted values at the sample means of the covariates, so that they may be viewed or plotted.

```
proc phreg data=SASUSER.SURVFINL;
  model days*status(0) = albumin edema prothom lbilirub y_age drug /
  SELECTION=FORWARD SLENTRY=.5 SEQUENTIAL;
  baseline survival=s;
run;
```

Figure 15.6   Batch file for sequential Cox regression survival analysis.

Output 15.4   SELECTED OUTPUT FOR SEQUENTIAL COX REGRESSION ANALYSIS.

The PHREG Procedure

Model Information

Data Set	SASUSER.SURVFINL
Dependent Variable	DAYS
Censoring Variable	STATUS
Censoring Value(s)	0
Ties Handling	BRESLOW

Summary of the Number of Event and Censored Values

Total	Event	Censored	Percent Censored
309	123	186	60.19

Step 5. Variable Y_AGE is entered. The model contains the following explanatory variables:

ALBUMIN EDEMA PROTHOM LBILIRUB Y_AGE

Model Fit Statistics

Criterion	Without Covariates	With Covariates
-2 LOG L	1255.756	1062.899
AIC	1255.756	1072.899
SBC	1255.756	1086.960

Testing Global Null Hypothesis: BETA=0

Test	Chi-Square	DF	Pr > ChiSq
Likelihood Ratio	192.8566	5	<.0001
Score	261.0975	5	<.0001
Wald	192.4954	5	<.0001

Step 6. Variable DRUG is entered. The model contains the following explanatory variables:

ALBUMIN EDEMA PROTHOM LBILIRUB Y_AGE DRUG

Model Fit Statistics

Criterion	Without Covariates	With Covariates
-2 LOG L	1255.756	1062.346
AIC	1255.756	1074.346
SBC	1255.756	1091.219

Testing Global Null Hypothesis: BETA=0

Test	Chi-Square	DF	Pr > ChiSq
Likelihood Ratio	193.4099	6	<.0001
Score	261.1999	6	<.0001
Wald	191.9437	6	<.0001

NOTE: All variables have been entered into the model.

Analysis of Maximum Likelihood Estimates

Variable	DF	Parameter Estimate	Standard Error	Wald Chi-Square	Pr > ChiSq	Hazard Ratio	Variable Label
ALBUMIN	1	-0.89397	0.24122	13.7349	0.0002	0.409	
EDEMA	1	0.74213	0.30826	5.7959	0.0161	2.100	
PROTHOM	1	0.30621	0.10360	8.7357	0.0031	1.358	
LBILIRUB	1	1.99360	0.23445	72.3041	<.0001	7.342	log10(BILIRUBI)
Y_AGE	1	0.03561	0.00890	16.0043	<.0001	1.036	
DRUG	1	0.13939	0.18716	0.5547	0.4564	1.150	

Plots of survivor functions are not available within SAS PHREG. However, they may be run through the plotting module once the predicted survival values are saved as per the syntax for the main run in a temporary file labeled PRED. From the **SAS/ASSIST: WorkPlace,** choose

> **Graphics**
> > **Plots**
> > > **Simple X*Y Plot...**

The **SAS/ASSIST: Simple X*Y** dialog box is filled in with the data set (**Table:** WORK.PRED), the **Vertical axis:** s, and the **Horizontal:** DAYS, as seen in Figure 15.7. Remaining choices are left with default values.

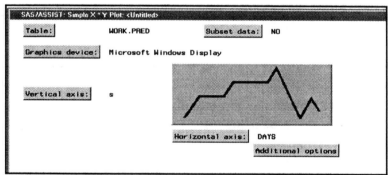

Figure 15.7   **SAS/ASSIST: Simple X*Y Plot** dialog box to plot survivor function at the mean of the covariates.

Clicking on the runner icon produces Figure 15.8.

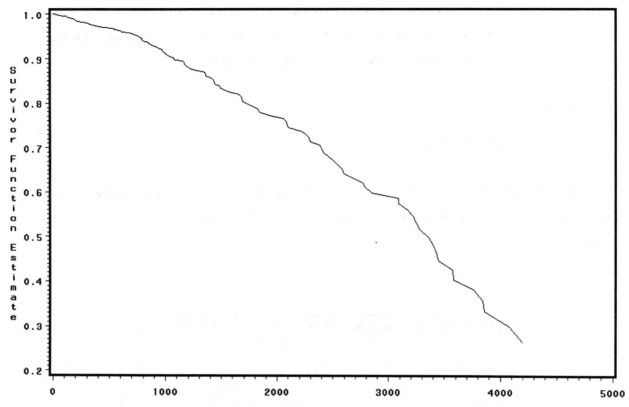

Figure 15.8   Survival function at mean of five covariates: serum albumen level, edema score, prothrombin time, logarithm of bilirubin level, and age in years.

212

Chapter 16. Time Series Analysis

This chapter demonstrates time series using SAS for Windows, for the complete example of Chapter 16 in *UMS*. The file to use is TIMESER.SAS7BDAT. This example examines the impact of a seat belt law enacted in 1985 in Illinois on incapacitating injuries.

16.1   EVALUATION OF ASSUMPTIONS

As reported in *UMS*, a look at the raw time series suggests the need for a logarithmic transform, as per Section 4.1.5. TIMESER.SAS7BDAT contains the transformed series, labeled LOG_INJ. No outliers are evident after transformation

16.2   BASELINE MODEL IDENTIFICATION AND ESTIMATION

ACF but not PACF PLOTS are available through the SAS/ASSIST menu system using the Time Series, Regression... module. Some trend adjustments are possible through the Seasonal Adjustment... module of **SAS/ASSIST Time Series**, which produces an output data set with the trend-adjusted series. However, the whole process is far simpler through syntax. Therefore batch processing used by typing the syntax of Tables 16.22 through 16.24 of *UMS* into the **Program Editor**.

16.3   BASELINE MODEL DIAGNOSIS

There is no convenient way to produce a normal probability plot through SAS/ASSIST, so the syntax of Figure 16.12 is typed into the **Program Editor.**

16.4   INTERVENTION ANALYSIS

Again, the ARIMA model of Section 16.7.4.1 of *UMS* is not readily available through SAS/ASSIST, so it is done through batch processing, using the syntax of Table 16.25. Medians for injuries before and after intervention are found through interactive data analysis (among other methods). The module is entered as per Section 3.3.3. Choosing

> **<u>A</u>nalyze**
>> **<u>D</u>istribution (Y)**

produces the **Distribution (Y)** dialog box of Figure 15.1 for choosing variables.

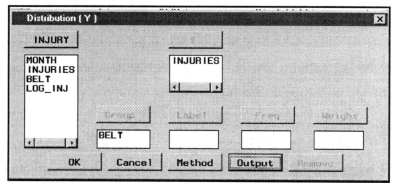

Figure 16.1   **Distribution (Y)** dialog box for time series
                interpretation.

Choose INJURIES as the **Y** variable and BELT as the **Group** variable. Clicking on the Output
button allows you to choose the desired descriptive statistics. Here the choice is ☑**Quantiles,** as seen in
Figure 16.2.

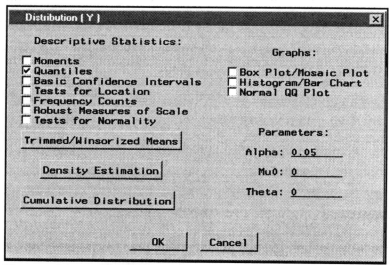

Figure 16.2   **Distribution(Y)** dialog box to choose Quantiles.

Clicking on **OK** returns the dialog box of Figure 16.1, where clicking on **OK** produces Figure 16.3, in
which the medians for each group (before and after intervention) are labeled 50% Med.

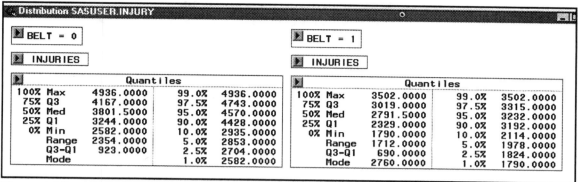

Figure 16.3   Medians for injuries before and after intervention.

Notes

Notes

Notes

Notes

Notes

Notes

Notes

Notes

Notes

Notes

Notes